McDougal Littell

World History

Ancient Civilizations

McDougal Littell
A-HOUGHTON MIFFLIN COMPANY

Evanston, Illinois • Boston • Dallas

Printed in the United States of America.

ISBN-13: 978-0-618-52997-1   ISBN-10: 0-618-52997-1

7 8 9 - VEI - 09 08

Reading Study Guide

Table of Contents

UNIT 4 ANCIENT ASIAN AND AMERICAN CIVILIZATIONS

UNIT 5 THE ROOTS OF WESTERN IDEAS

UNIT 6 THE WORLD OF ANCIENT ROME

How to Use This *Reading Study Guide*

The purpose of this *Reading Study Guide* is to help you read and understand your history textbook, *World History: Ancient Civilizations.* You can use this *Reading Study Guide* in two ways.

1. Use the *Reading Study Guide* side-by-side with your history book.

• Turn to the lesson that you are going to read in the textbook. Then, next to the book, put the pages from the *Reading Study Guide* that accompany that lesson. All of the heads in the *Reading Study Guide* match the heads in the textbook.

• Use the *Reading Study Guide* to help you read and organize the information in the textbook.

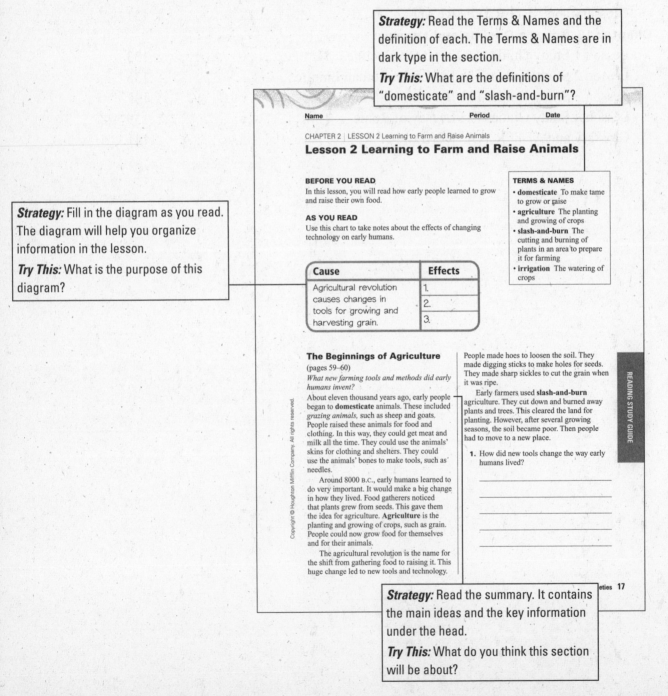

Strategy: Read the Terms & Names and the definition of each. The Terms & Names are in dark type in the section.

Try This: What are the definitions of "domesticate" and "slash-and-burn"?

Strategy: Fill in the diagram as you read. The diagram will help you organize information in the lesson.

Try This: What is the purpose of this diagram?

Name   Period   Date

CHAPTER 2 | LESSON 2 Learning to Farm and Raise Animals

Lesson 2 Learning to Farm and Raise Animals

BEFORE YOU READ
In this lesson, you will read how early people learned to grow and raise their own food.

AS YOU READ
Use this chart to take notes about the effects of changing technology on early humans.

Cause	Effects
Agricultural revolution causes changes in tools for growing and harvesting grain.	1.
	2.
	3.

TERMS & NAMES
• **domesticate** To make tame to grow or raise
• **agriculture** The planting and growing of crops
• **slash-and-burn** The cutting and burning of plants in an area to prepare it for farming
• **irrigation** The watering of crops

The Beginnings of Agriculture
(pages 59–60)
What new farming tools and methods did early humans invent?
About eleven thousand years ago, early people began to **domesticate** animals. These included *grazing animals,* such as sheep and goats. People raised these animals for food and clothing. In this way, they could get meat and milk all the time. They could use the animals' skins for clothing and shelters. They could use the animals' bones to make tools, such as needles.

Around 8000 B.C., early humans learned to do very important. It would make a big change in how they lived. Food gatherers noticed that plants grew from seeds. This gave them the idea for agriculture. **Agriculture** is the planting and growing of crops, such as grain. People could now grow food for themselves and for their animals.

The agricultural revolution is the name for the shift from gathering food to raising it. This huge change led to new tools and technology.

People made hoes to loosen the soil. They made digging sticks to make holes for seeds. They made sharp sickles to cut the grain when it was ripe.

Early farmers used **slash-and-burn** agriculture. They cut down and burned away plants and trees. This cleared the land for planting. However, after several growing seasons, the soil became poor. Then people had to move to a new place.

1. How did new tools change the way early humans lived?

_____

_____

_____

_____

eties **17**

Strategy: Read the summary. It contains the main ideas and the key information under the head.

Try This: What do you think this section will be about?

2. Use the *Reading Study Guide* to study for tests on the textbook.

- Reread the summary of every chapter.
- Review the definitions of the Terms & Names in the *Reading Study Guide.*
- Review the diagram of information that you filled out as you read the summaries.
- Review your answers to questions.

Name _____ Period _____ Date _____

READING STUDY GUIDE CONTINUED

Settlements Begin
(pages 60–61)

Why did villages develop?

New tools improved farming. People could raise more food than before. The soil lasted longer, too. People did not have to move every few years. They began to *develop* permanent villages.

River valleys had especially *fertile* soil. This soil was better than soil made by slashing and burning. Farmers wanted to settle where the soil was so rich. They started small villages near their fields. Villages grew to hold several thousand people. The people lived in simple homes. These dwelling were made from mud, bricks, logs, and hides.

There were some disadvantages to living in a village. There was a greater chance of fire and disease. Villages near rivers were in danger from floods, too. However, living in a village made life easier in some ways. There was plenty of food. Also, people living in larger groups could better defend themselves from nomad attacks.

2. How did the agricultural revolution change life for early humans?

_____

_____

_____

Farming Develops in Many Places
(pages 61–62)

Where did farming develop?

The agricultural revolution did not happen in just one place. It happened at the same time in different parts of the world. Early humans farmed where there was a steady source of water. River valleys were especially good places.

People farmed along rivers such as the Huang He in China. They farmed on the Nile in Africa, too. Farmers on the Nile were among the first to use **irrigation** to water their crops. They built dikes and canals to move the water.

In the Americas, people began farming later than in other places. They also tended to farm in the uplands, instead of along rivers. The uplands are high, flat areas. Early humans in the Americas invented ways to farm in their environment. They made terraces to adapt the steep land for growing crops. On these flat spaces, they grew corn, beans, potatoes, and squash.

3. How did early humans in the Americas adapt the land for farming?

_____

_____

_____

Strategy: Underline main ideas and key information as you read.

Try This: read the summary under the head "Farming Develops in Many Places." Underline information that you think is important.

Strategy: Answer the question at the end of each part.

Try This: Write an answer to Question 3.

At the end of every chapter in the *Reading Study Guide,* you will find a Glossary and a section called After You Read. The Glossary gives definitions of important words used in the chapter. After You Read is a two-page chapter review. Use After You Read to identify those parts of the chapter that you need to study more for the test on the chapter.

Name _____ Period _____ Date _____

CHAPTER 2 | The Earliest Human Societies

Chapter 2 The Earliest Human Societies

Glossary/After You Read

band a group of people or animals acting together
community a group of people with close ties living in one area
apply to put into action or to use
spirit the part of a being believed to control thinking and feeling; the soul
grazing animal an animal that feeds growing grass

develop to grow or cause to grow
fertile good for plants to grow in
potter a person who makes objects, such as pots, from moist clay hardened by heat
encourage to help to bring about; foster
inhabitant a resident of a place
suggest to show indirectly

Terms & Names
A. Circle the name or term that best com[...]

1. The _____ moved around in sear[...]

   artisan   nomad   social clas[...]

2. Around 8000 B.C., people got the ide[...]

   irrigation   migration   agric[...]

3. The _____ of grain hel[...]

   hunter-gatherer   religion[...]

4. Stone tools were some of the first us[...]

   irrigation   technology   ag[...]

5. Early humans used _____

   specialization   government

B. Write the letter of the word that best n[...]

_____ **6.** To tame for raising or growing[...]

_____ **7.** A skill in one kind of work[...]

_____ **8.** Keeps order and provides leade[...]

_____ **9.** The worship of God, gods, or s[...]

_____ **10.** A person trained at a skill or c[...]

READING STUDY GUIDE

Name _____ Period _____

READING STUDY GUIDE CONTINUED

Main Ideas

11. How did early hunter-gatherers interact with their environment?
_____
_____

12. How did tools help early people to survive?
_____
_____

13. What was the agricultural revolution?
_____
_____

14. In what ways did agriculture change how people lived?
_____
_____

15. What were some basic features of a complex village?
_____
_____

Thinking Critically

16. Making Inferences How does technology give people more control over their environment?
_____
_____

17. Understanding Cause and Effect Why would a village have a greater need for government than a hunter-gatherer band?
_____
_____

Strategy: Review all of the of Terms & Names before completing Parts A and B of After You Read.
Try This: Use the *Reading Study Guide* for Chapter 1 to answer Questions A 1–5.

Strategy: Review the chapter summaries before completing the Main Ideas questions. Write a complete sentence for every answer.
Try This: In your own words, what is Question 11 asking for?

Strategy: Write one or two paragraphs for every Thinking Critically question.
Try This: In your own words, what is Question 1 asking for?

CHAPTER 1 | LESSON 1 The World's Geography

Lesson 1 The World's Geography

BEFORE YOU READ

In this lesson, you will learn about the landforms and bodies of water that shape Earth and how geography affects where and how people live.

AS YOU READ

Use a diagram like the one below to summarize each section of Lesson 1. Identify the main idea and important details in each section to complete your summary.

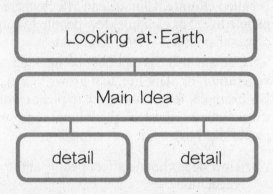

TERMS & NAMES

- **geography** the study of Earth and its people
- **continent** one of the seven large landmasses that make up Earth
- **landform** a naturally formed feature on Earth's surface
- **climate** the weather conditions in a place over a long period of time
- **vegetation** plant life

Looking at Earth

(pages 9–10)

What do geographers study?

The study of Earth and the people living on it is called **geography.** People who study geography are called geographers. They study the land and water on Earth. They also study how people live on Earth.

Earth is made up of seven large landmasses called **continents.** The seven continents are Asia, Africa, North America, South America, Antarctica, Europe, and Australia.

The continents lie on large plates that move. The movements form mountains and volcanoes and cause earthquakes. The movements also help reshape Earth.

Australia and Antarctica are islands. An island is a **landform.** A landform is a naturally formed feature on Earth's surface. Other kinds of landforms are mountains, plateaus, and

plains. Plateaus are high, flat areas. Plains are large, level areas of grasslands.

About three-fourths of Earth is covered by water. The largest bodies of water are called oceans. The four major oceans are the Pacific Ocean, the Atlantic Ocean, the Indian Ocean, and the Arctic Ocean. Rivers and lakes are smaller bodies of water on Earth.

1. What kinds of landforms and bodies of water make up Earth?

_____

_____

_____

Themes of Geography

(page 11)

What are the five themes of geography?

To help understand the world and how people fit in it, geographers use five themes.

- Location answers the question, Where is it? Location identifies the exact spot where a place is.

- Place answers the question, What is it like? Place tells about an area's physical features. It also tells about the people who live there, including their language, religion, and government.

- Region answers the question, How are places the same and how are they different? Region compares the physical and human features of places.

- Movement answers the question, How do people, goods, and ideas move from one place to another?

- Human-Environment Interaction answers the question, How do people interact with the physical world? It tells how people use and change the environment around them.

2. What five themes do geographers use to help them understand the world and how people live in it?

_____

_____

_____

How Environment Affects People

(pages 11–12)

How does climate affect people's lives?

The kind of environment you live in has an effect on the way you live. For example, you wear a coat in cold weather, and you dress in light clothing in warm weather. However, different people may have different ways of adapting, or adjusting, to the same area.

The temperature and conditions in a place at a particular time is called weather. The weather conditions over a long period of time is called **climate.** Climate can affect where people live. For example, few people live in places that have a very cold climate.

Climate also has an effect on the kinds of **vegetation,** or plant life, that grows in a place. For example, few plants grow in places with a dry climate. However, thick jungles grow in places that have a hot, wet climate.

3. How does climate affect people and vegetation?

_____

_____

_____

CHAPTER 1 | LESSON 2 How Maps Help Us Study History

Lesson 2 How Maps Help Us Study History

BEFORE YOU READ

In this lesson, you will learn how globes and maps are used to study Earth and the people who live on it.

AS YOU READ

Use the example of the Venn diagram below to make comparisons in Lesson 2. Draw two different diagrams and use them to compare maps and globes and two kinds of maps. In the middle section of each diagram, include the ways that maps and globes or the two kinds of maps are the same. In the outer circles, list the ways that the two items you are comparing are different.

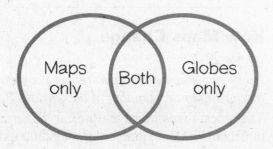

Maps only   Both   Globes only

TERMS & NAMES

- **longitude** imaginary lines that measure distances east and west of the prime meridian
- **latitude** imaginary lines that measure distances north and south of the equator
- **hemisphere** half of a globe
- **political map** map that shows features people have created
- **physical map** map that shows the landforms and bodies of water found in particular areas
- **thematic map** map that shows certain information about a place

The Geographer's Tools

(pages 15–18)

What are the geographer's tools?

Geographers use globes and maps to represent Earth. Because a globe is round, it looks more like Earth. A globe shows exactly how continents and oceans look on Earth. It also shows the real shapes, locations, and sizes of the landforms and bodies of water.

A map is a flat representation of Earth. It is not as accurate as a globe because the surface of Earth is distorted when it is flattened to make a map. So a map does not show the surface of Earth as it really looks. However, most people like to use maps. This is because you can measure distances on a map more easily than on a globe. You can see the world all at one time on a map. Also, it is easier to carry a map because it can be folded.

Most maps include nine features that help to understand what is shown on the maps.

- The title tells what the map is about.
- A compass rose shows the directions.
- Symbols represent such things as cities.
- A map legend explains what the symbols and colors on the map mean.
- Lines of **longitude** measure distances east and west of the prime meridian.
- Lines of **latitude** measure distances north and south of the equator.
- A scale is used to figure out distances between places on a map.
- Labels tell the names of landforms and bodies of water.
- Colors show different kinds of information on a map.

Maps distort Earth's surface, so mapmakers try to control the distortion by using different projections. A projection is a way of showing Earth's curved surface on a flat map. The Mercator projection shows the continents as they look on the globe. However it stretches out the lands that are near the north and south poles. The homolosine projection shows the sizes of the landmasses correctly. However, the distances are not accurate. The Robinson projection is often used in textbooks. It shows the true shapes and sizes of the continents and oceans. But landforms near the poles look flat.

To study Earth, geographers divide it into **hemispheres,** or equal halves. The half of Earth north of the equator is the Northern Hemisphere. The half south of the equator is the Southern Hemisphere. The imaginary line that divides Earth east from west is the prime meridian. The half of Earth east of this line is the Eastern Hemisphere. The half west of this line is the Western Hemisphere.

Geographers use lines of latitude and lines of longitude to find points on Earth. The point where a line of latitude crosses a line of longitude is the exact spot on Earth where a place is located. Absolute location is given using the numbers of the latitude and longitude lines. They are measured in degrees. Every place on Earth has only one absolute location.

1. How do symbols and scales help us read and understand maps?

_____

_____

Different Maps for Different Purposes

(pages 19–21)

What different maps do we use to see natural and human-made features and to understand patterns?

There are three kinds of maps. A **political map** shows the features that people make. These features include cities, states, and countries. You can use a political map to find

things such as where a place is located and how many people live in a place.

A **physical map** shows what Earth's surface looks like. It shows landforms and bodies of water. Colors are used to show elevations, or height of the land. You can use a physical map to find out if an area has mountains or to find out which direction rivers flow.

A **thematic map** shows certain information about a place. You can use a thematic map to find such things as the climate of a place, the languages people speak in a region, and the battles that took place during a war.

2. What kind of map would you use to find out what countries are located in Asia?

_____

How Maps Change

(pages 22–23)

How have maps changed to reflect people's increasing understanding of the world?

The oldest maps we have were carved on clay tablets by the Babylonians around 2300 B.C. A Greek astronomer in the second century A.D. wrote a work called *Geography*. It had instructions on how to make maps.

In the Middle Ages, Arab and Chinese mapmakers made accurate maps of parts of the world. They used their knowledge of astronomy and mathematics to make their maps. European maps improved in the mid-1500s. At that time Gerhardus Mercator, a mapmaker, showed the curved surface of Earth on a flat map. This is the Mercator projection.

Maps today are made by using the satellites of the Global Positioning System (GPS). The satellites go around Earth. Receivers identify the satellites' signals and use them to figure out location.

3. How did the ancient Greeks contribute to mapmaking?

_____

_____

Lesson 3 How Archaeologists Study the Past

BEFORE YOU READ

In this lesson, you will learn how archaeologists and other scientists learn about early people and what life was like long ago.

AS YOU READ

As you read Lesson 3, use a diagram like the one below to identify the main idea of each section.

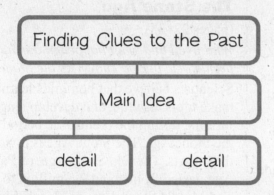

TERMS & NAMES
- **artifact** human-made object
- **fossil** remains of early life preserved in the ground
- **hominid** human and humanlike creatures that walk on two feet
- **Paleolithic Age** the Old Stone Age
- **Mesolithic Age** the Middle Stone Age
- **Neolithic Age** the New Stone Age

Finding Clues to the Past

(pages 27–28)

How do archaeologists uncover the story of early peoples?

Archaeologists are scientists who study early people by digging up and studying early settlements. They look for bones and other evidence that might tell them about what life was like long ago.

Archaeologists work with other scientists. Some of these scientists help to figure out when **artifacts,** or human-made objects, were made and what they were used for.

Anthropologists are scientists who study culture. Culture is the way of life of a group of people. Culture includes the beliefs that people have, the language they speak, and the ways they do things. This information helps

archaeologists make connections between the past and the present.

Fossils also give information about early people. Fossils are the remains of early life preserved in the ground. They include pieces of teeth and bones. Archaeologists use special techniques to figure out the ages of ancient fossils and artifacts.

1. How do anthropologists help archaeologists learn about early people?

_____

_____

_____

READING STUDY GUIDE CONTINUED

The Search for Early Humans

(pages 29–31)

What have archaeologists learned about early humans from the evidence they have found?

Most scientists believe that humans began in Africa. Some of the earliest humanlike beings are called australopithecines. These beings and others that walk on two feet are called **hominids.** Humans are also hominids. Scientists think that australopithecines learned to walk about 4.5 million years ago in East Africa.

Scientists believe that about 2.5 million years ago a hominid called *Homo habilis* also appeared in East Africa. These hominids used stone tools to cut meat and to crack open bones.

Scientists believe that about 1.6 million years ago a hominid called *Homo erectus,* appeared. This hominid was able to walk upright.

Human culture, or way of life, developed with the appearance of *Homo sapiens.* Early *Homo sapiens* created cave paintings and made sharper tools. Eventually, they began to farm, write, and build villages. Some modern *Homo sapiens* called *Cro-Magnons* appeared about 35,000 years ago. They moved from North Africa to Europe and Asia.

The Leakeys, a family of British archaeologists, have made many important contributions. They began looking for early human fossils in East Africa in the 1930s. In 1960, they found some fossils of *Homo habilis* in East Africa. The Leakeys showed that *Homo habilis* was our ancestor.

In 1974, an American archaeologist discovered the nearly complete skeleton of an australopithecine that was named Lucy.

The Leakeys' son discovered the skeleton of a *Homo erectus* in 1984. In recent years, scientists have found the skeletons of other hominids.

2. Why was the work of the Leakeys important?

_____

_____

_____

The Stone Age

(pages 32–33)

Who lived and what happened during the prehistoric period known as the Stone Age?

Scientists believe that hominids learned to make tools, use fire, and develop language and farming during the prehistoric period known as the Stone Age. The Stone Age is divided into three parts. The Old Stone Age, or **Paleolithic Age,** lasted from about 2.5 million to 8000 B.C. The Middle Stone Age, or **Mesolithic Age,** lasted between 10,000 and 6000 B.C. The New Stone Age, or **Neolithic Age,** lasted from about 8000 to 3000 B.C.

Farming began in the Neolithic Age. It changed people's lives. People did not have to wander from place to place to find food. They began to settle down and build communities.

3. How did farming change people's lives?

_____

_____

_____

READING STUDY GUIDE

CHAPTER 1 | LESSON 4 HOW HISTORIANS STUDY THE PAST

Lesson 4 How Historians Study the Past

BEFORE YOU READ

In this lesson, you will learn what methods historians use to study the past.

AS YOU READ

Use this web diagram to record the three main jobs of historians.

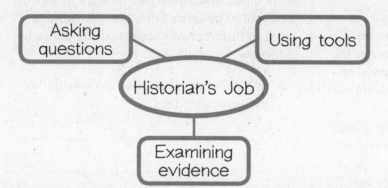

TERMS & NAMES

• **primary source** something written or created by a person who witnessed a historical event

• **secondary source** something written after a historical event by a person who did not witness the event

• **oral history** all the unwritten verbal accounts of events

Understanding the Past

(pages 39–40)

What questions do historians ask to help them understand the past?

We study world history because what happened to a society affects what will happen today and in the future. History is more than just studying what happened in the past. When you study a historical event, you also study a society's culture, religion, politics, and economics.

Historians look for causes and effects that help to explain how and why events happened. They try to see the past through the eyes of the people who lived it.

When they study the past, historians ask themselves questions. The answers to the questions help historians draw conclusions

about the past. For example, historians ask questions such as how societies are similar and different. They also ask how leaders governed societies.

1. What do historians do when they study the past?

   _____

   _____

   _____

   _____

READING STUDY GUIDE

The Tools of History 11

READING STUDY GUIDE CONTINUED

The Historian's Tools

(pages 40–41)

What methods do historians use to help them answer questions about what happened in the past?

Historians use tools to help them do their job. Some of these tools are **primary sources.** A primary source is something written or created by a person who saw a historical event. Letters, diaries, speeches, and photographs are examples of primary sources. Artifacts such as tools are also primary sources.

Other tools that historians use are **secondary sources.** They are written after a historical event by people who did not see the event. Books and paintings that are based on primary sources and appear after an event are examples of secondary sources.

Yet another tool that historians use is **oral history.** This is made up of all the unwritten verbal accounts of events. Historians depend on oral history when studying cultures that have no written records. Oral histories include the stories, customs, and songs that people in a culture have passed down from generation to generation. /

2. What is the difference between primary and secondary sources?

_____

_____

_____

_____

How Knowledge of the Past Changes

(pages 42–43)

What steps do historians take as they answer historical questions?

Historians use evidence from primary and secondary sources and oral histories to answer their questions. They have to choose what information is most important and trustworthy as evidence.

Historical evidence is not always simple. Sometimes what historians thought to be true turns out to be false. Sometimes historians come to different conclusions using the same evidence.

3. What do historians have to do with the evidence they find?

_____

_____

_____

_____

CHAPTER 1 | The Tools Of History

Chapter 1 The Tools of History

Glossary/After You Read

indicate show or point out

influence to have an effect or impact on something

interaction when two or more things affect each other

remains parts of a dead body

symbol a thing that stands for something else

system group of things that work together as a whole

theme topics of discussion

Terms & Names

A. Circle the name or term that best completes each sentence.

1. The large landmasses on Earth are called _____.

   continents   oceans   plateaus

2. A _____ is a naturally formed feature on Earth's surface.

   climate   landform   continent

3. A _____ map shows features that people have created.

   political   physical   thematic

4. Archaeologists study _____, which are remains of early life preserved in the ground.

   artifacts   hominids   fossils

5. Something that is written or created by a person who witnessed a historical event is a(n) _____.

   primary source   secondary source   oral history

B. Write the letter of the term that matches the description.

_____ **6.** What geographers use to help them understand the world and how people fit in it

_____ **7.** The place where most scientists believe humans began

_____ **8.** The study of Earth and its people

_____ **9.** A way of showing Earth's curved surface on a flat map

_____ **10.** The largest bodies of water on Earth

_____ **11.** The period in history when farming began

a. geography

b. North America

c. oceans

d. five themes

e. Old Stone Age

f. projection

g. Africa

h. New Stone Age

READING STUDY GUIDE

READING STUDY GUIDE CONTINUED

Main Ideas

12. What is the advantage of using maps over globes?

_____

_____

13. How do geographers find an absolute location on Earth?

_____

_____

14. Why do geographers use different kinds of maps?

_____

_____

15. What developments occurred during the Stone Age?

_____

_____

16. What three tool do historians use to help them answer questions about the past?

_____

_____

Thinking Critically

17. Making Inferences How does the environment affect the way you live?

_____

_____

18. Assessing Credibility of Sources Why do historians have to evaluate the primary and secondary sources they use to answer their questions?

_____

_____

CHAPTER 2 | LESSON 1 Hunters and Gatherers

Lesson 1 Hunters and Gatherers

BEFORE YOU READ

In this lesson, you will read how early humans got food, what tools they used, and how they lived.

AS YOU READ

Use this diagram to take notes about how early people lived.

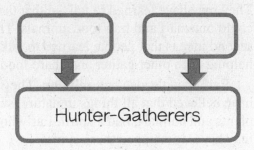

TERMS & NAMES

- **hunter-gatherer** People who hunt animals and gather plants for food
- **nomad** A person who moves from place to place
- **migration** The act of moving from place to place
- **technology** All the ways in which people apply knowledge, tools, and inventions to meet their needs
- **religion** The worship of God, gods, or spirits

Early Humans' Way of Life

(pages 51–53)

How did early humans interact with the environment?

Early humans lived very closely with nature. They were **hunter-gatherers,** which means they ate what they could get in their own environment. Men hunted and fished. Women gathered nuts and berries. When the food in one place was gone, the people moved to a new place.

These early people were **nomads** who moved around. They lived in small groups called bands. A *band* could include several families or about 30 people. These people did not build permanent homes. Some took shelter in caves they found. Others made simple shelters from branches or animal skins.

Some hunter-gatherer bands returned to the same places at the turn of the seasons. At certain times of the year, they would join other bands to form a bigger *community*. At these times they might tell stories and meet friends. They would also find people to marry.

Some hunter-gatherer bands moved far from their original lands. They might have followed the **migrations** of the animals they hunted. By 15,000 B.C., these early people had spread around the world, even as far as the Americas.

Migrating groups brought tools and new ideas with them. However, a new group could seem threatening. They might be too different. This could sometimes cause fighting between groups.

1. Why did early humans move around often?

_____

_____

_____

_____

_____

READING STUDY GUIDE

The Development of Tools

(page 53)

What were some tools created by early humans?

Around 500,000 years ago people learned to make and use fire. It gave them heat and light. It let them cook food and protected them from animals. Early people also used fire to help make tools.

Tools are a very ancient kind of **technology.** Simple tool making goes back at least 2 million years. Early people made stone tools for cutting. Other tools were used to make holes in leather and wood. These tools included axes, awls, and drills.

Later, humans made more complex tools, such as wooden bows. They also made arrows and spears with flint tips. Flint is a kind of stone that can be shaped to have a very sharp edge.

Humans used these tools to hunt and butcher animals for food. They also used them to make simple shelters and clothing. Humans learned to apply their tool technology to control their environment.

2. Name some tools early humans made.

_____

_____

_____

_____

Early Human Culture

(pages 54–55)

What kind of culture did early humans create?

Language, religion, and art are special behaviors. They are what make humans different from other creatures. They are also part of human culture.

There are two ideas about how humans developed language. The first idea is that people needed to work together during a hunt. They may have learned to talk so that they could outsmart and trap food animals. The second idea is that people learned to talk while helping each other gather and share food.

Early people also had **religion.** They may have believed that all things in nature, such as plants and animals, had a spirit. Early humans may have worshipped these spirits.

Early human art has been found all around the world. Some of it may have had religious meanings. Early people made art they could carry, such as jewelry and small statues. They sang, danced and played music. They told stories, too.

Early humans also painted on cave and rock walls. More than 200 sites of early cave art have been found in Europe. These paintings show colorful images of bulls, horses, and bison. Some scientists think this art honors the spirits of the animals because they were killed for food.

3. What were the main features of early human culture?

_____

_____

READING STUDY GUIDE

CHAPTER 2 | LESSON 2 Learning to Farm and Raise Animals

Lesson 2 Learning to Farm and Raise Animals

BEFORE YOU READ

In this lesson, you will read how early people learned to grow and raise their own food.

AS YOU READ

Use this chart to take notes about the effects of changing technology on early humans.

Cause	Effects
Agricultural revolution causes changes in tools for growing and harvesting grain.	1.
	2.
	3.

TERMS & NAMES

- **domesticate** To make tame to grow or raise
- **agriculture** The planting and growing of crops
- **slash-and-burn** The cutting and burning of plants in an area to prepare it for farming
- **irrigation** The watering of crops

The Beginnings of Agriculture

(pages 59–60)

What new farming tools and methods did early humans invent?

About eleven thousand years ago, early people began to **domesticate** animals. These included *grazing animals,* such as sheep and goats. People raised these animals for food and clothing. In this way, they could get meat and milk all the time. They could use the animals' skins for clothing and shelters. They could use the animals' bones to make tools, such as needles.

Around 8000 B.C., early humans learned to do very important. It would make a big change in how they lived. Food gatherers noticed that plants grew from seeds. This gave them the idea for agriculture. **Agriculture** is the planting and growing of crops, such as grain. People could now grow food for themselves and for their animals.

The agricultural revolution is the name for the shift from gathering food to raising it. This huge change led to new tools and technology.

People made hoes to loosen the soil. They made digging sticks to make holes for seeds. They made sharp sickles to cut the grain when it was ripe.

Early farmers used **slash-and-burn** agriculture. They cut down and burned away plants and trees. This cleared the land for planting. However, after several growing seasons, the soil became poor. Then people had to move to a new place.

1. How did new tools change the way early humans lived?

_____

_____

_____

_____

READING STUDY GUIDE

Settlements Begin

(pages 60–61)

Why did villages develop?

New tools improved farming. People could raise more food than before. The soil lasted longer, too. People did not have to move every few years. They began to *develop* permanent villages.

River valleys had especially *fertile* soil. This soil was better than soil made by slashing and burning. Farmers wanted to settle where the soil was so rich. They started small villages near their fields. Villages grew to hold several thousand people. The people lived in simple homes. These dwellings were made from mud, bricks, logs, and hides.

There were some disadvantages to living in a village. There was a greater chance of fire and disease. Villages near rivers were in danger from floods, too. However, living in a village made life easier in some ways. There was plenty of food. Also, people living in larger groups could better defend themselves from nomad attacks.

2. How did the agricultural revolution change life for early humans?

_____

_____

_____

Farming Develops in Many Places

(pages 61–62)

Where did farming develop?

The agricultural revolution did not happen in just one place. It happened at the same time in different parts of the world. Early humans farmed where there was a steady source of water. River valleys were especially good places.

People farmed along rivers such as the Huang He in China. They farmed on the Nile in Africa, too. Farmers on the Nile were among the first to use **irrigation** to water their crops. They built dikes and canals to move the water.

In the Americas, people began farming later than in other places. They also tended to farm in the uplands, instead of along rivers. The uplands are high, flat areas. Early humans in the Americas invented ways to farm in their environment. They made terraces to adapt the steep land for growing crops. On these flat spaces, they grew corn, beans, potatoes, and squash.

3. How did early humans in the Americas adapt the land for farming?

_____

_____

_____

READING STUDY GUIDE

CHAPTER 2 | LESSON 3 The First Communities

Lesson 3 The First Communities

BEFORE YOU READ

In this lesson, you will read how simple villages grew into more complex communities.

AS YOU READ

Use this concept web to take notes about the first communities.

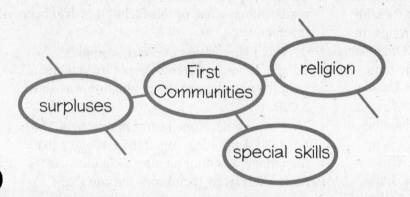

TERMS & NAMES

- **surplus** More than is needed to live
- **specialization** A skill in one kind of work
- **artisan** A person trained in a skill or craft
- **social class** A group of people with similar background and status
- **government** A system for creating order and giving leadership

Villages Around the World

(pages 65–66)

How did farming villages develop?

Living in a village was much different from living in a nomad band. Villagers were settled. They did not move around. They also did not have to depend on hunting and gathering for food. Many did not even have to farm.

This is because better farm technology led to food **surpluses.** Farmers sometimes grew more grain than they needed to feed their families. They grew more than the village needed, too. This was an economic surplus.

There were other surpluses in addition to food. There might be a surplus of sheep's wool, for example. Surplus food and goods helped the villages to live through bad times.

A food surplus meant that not everyone had to work to grow food. Many people could spend their time doing something else. They developed **specializations** in skills other than farming. They learned crafts such as making pots or weaving cloth. Everyone wanted pots and cloth. *Potters* and weavers could trade the goods they made for food.

Other people in the village had different skills. They were believed to be holy. These shamans were linked to the spirit world. It was their job to explain what happened in nature, such as a fire or a bad harvest. They could also be healers. Later, these holy people became priests in the first cities.

1. How did surpluses lead to specialization?

_____

_____

_____

READING STUDY GUIDE

Simple Villages Grow More Complex

(pages 66–67)

How did life in villages become more complex?

Surpluses *encouraged* the growth of villages. Extra food and other goods meant that more people could live together. Surpluses led to the growth of trade, too. People in one village might trade their surplus food. In return, they would get another village's surplus tools.

Specialization increased. Potters, carpenters, weavers and other **artisans** spent a long time learning their skills. Those with similar skills started to form into groups. In this way, **social classes** developed. Other social classes grew around groups with the same backgrounds, training, and income. These included farmers, priests, and rulers.

As early communities grew, people began to want laws. They also wanted leadership to keep order and settle arguments. This led to a simple kind of **government.** Early governments were formed to make villages safer and more stable.

Soon simple villages became complex villages. They were larger and more varied. They had more people, ideas, and skills. They also had more needs.

2. What are two ways in which simple villages became more complex?

   _____

   _____

   _____

Life in a Complex Village

(pages 67–69)

How did life in a complex village compare with that in a simple village?

A complex village was not like a modern city. In early times, most villages had only a few hundred *inhabitants.* A complex village might have 5,000. It would be very small today.

Complex villages were different from modern towns in other ways. They did not have electricity. They did not have public buses or trains. They did not have skyscrapers or paved roads, either. None of this technology had been invented yet.

Catal Huyuk was one early complex village. It was in Turkey. People lived there at least 8,000 years ago. Its population was about 5,000.

Farming developed early in this area. The bones of water birds found there suggest that the village was built on marshy land. Farmers most likely grew their crops outside the village.

Catal Huyuk may have been small. However, its ruins show that the people lived complex lives. They lived in permanent houses made of brick. The houses were clustered together. Their floor plans were much alike. Other buildings were shrines. They had religious art on the walls. There is also evidence of offerings to the gods in these places.

People in Catal Huyuk had special skills. They created luxury goods such as mirrors and beads. They made cloth, wooden containers, and pottery, too. Artisans created murals on many of the buildings. This village was an important center of trade and culture.

3. What were some features of a complex village?

   _____

   _____

   _____

Chapter 2 The Earliest Human Societies

Glossary/After You Read

band a group of people or animals acting together

community a group of people with close ties living in one area

apply to put into action or to use

spirit the part of a being believed to control thinking and feeling; the soul

grazing animal an animal that feeds on growing grass

develop to grow or cause to grow

fertile good for plants to grow in

potter a person who makes objects, such as pots, from moist clay hardened by heat

encourage to help to bring about; foster

inhabitant a resident of a place

suggest to show indirectly

Terms & Names

A. Circle the name or term that best completes each sentence.

1. The _____ moved around in search of food.

    artisan   nomad   social class

2. Around 8000 B.C., people got the idea of _____ and began to plant seeds.

    irrigation   migration   agriculture

3. The _____ of grain helped the village to survive during bad times.

    hunter-gatherer   religion   surplus

4. Stone tools were some of the first uses of _____.

    irrigation   technology   agriculture

5. Early humans used _____ to clear the land for farming.

    specialization   government   slash-and-burn

B. Write the letter of the word that best matches the description below.

____ **6.** To tame for raising or growing

____ **7.** A skill in one kind of work

____ **8.** Keeps order and provides leadership

____ **9.** The worship of God, gods, or spirits

____ **10.** A person trained at a skill or craft

a. government

b. domesticate

c. religion

d. specialization

e. artisan

f. social class

READING STUDY GUIDE

READING STUDY GUIDE CONTINUED

Main Ideas

11. How did early hunter-gatherers interact with their environment?

_____

_____

12. How did tools help early people to survive?

_____

_____

13. What was the agricultural revolution?

_____

_____

14. In what ways did agriculture change how people lived?

_____

_____

15. What were some basic features of a complex village?

_____

_____

Thinking Critically

16. Making Inferences How does technology give people more control over their environment?

_____

_____

17. Understanding Cause and Effect Why would a village have a greater need for government than a hunter-gatherer band?

_____

_____

CHAPTER 3 | LESSON 1 Geography of Mesopotamia

Lesson 1 Geography of Mesopotamia

BEFORE YOU READ

In Lesson 1, you will learn how the Tigris and Euphrates rivers made the Mesopotamian region a good place for settlement.

AS YOU READ

After you read Lesson 1, write a sentence or two summarizing each of the three main sections. Use a chart like this one to record your summaries.

TERMS & NAMES
• **Mesopotamia** the region where the Tigris and Euphrates rivers flow
• **floodplain** the flat land bordering the banks of a river
• **silt** the fine soil deposited by rivers
• **semiarid** climate that is hot and fairly dry
• **drought** a period when not enough rain and snow fall
• **surplus** more than is needed

Geography of Mesopotamia
The rivers of Mesopotamia were important because . . .
Mesopotamians watered their crops by . . .
Because of a lack of resources, . . .

The Land Between Two Rivers

(pages 83–84)

How did the land between the Tigris and Euphrates rivers support agriculture?

The Tigris and Euphrates rivers start in the mountains of southwest Asia. The region between the rivers was called **Mesopotamia.** The land here was mostly flat with small plants. The rivers provided water and were important for travel. It was easier to travel by boat than over land. There were very few roads on land. Boats could carry heavier loads. The currents helped move the boats down river.

Rain and melting snow in the mountains caused the rivers to get bigger. The water in the rivers picked up soil as it flowed down the mountains. When this water reached the plains, it overflowed into the floodplain. A **floodplain** is the flat land that borders the banks of a river. As the water covered the floodplain, the fine soil it carried settled on the land. The fine soil deposited by rivers is called **silt.** The silt was fertile, making it good for growing crops.

The climate in Mesopotamia is **semiarid.** Usually less than 10 inches of rain a year fall there, and summers are hot. Even though

READING STUDY GUIDE

the region was dry, the rivers and fertile soil made it good for farming. By 4000 B.C., many farming villages developed in southern Mesopotamia.

1. How were the Tigris and Euphrates rivers important to Mesopotamia?

_____

_____

_____

Controlling Water by Irrigation

(pages 84–85)

How did the climate affect farmers?

People in Mesopotamia could not predict when the rivers would flood each year. As a result, they could not predict when to plant crops. The people also could not predict the size of the flooding. That depended on how much snow or rain fell in the mountains. Too much rain could cause huge floods that washed everything away. If too little rain or snow fell, there might not be any flooding at all.

Semiarid regions sometimes experience a **drought.** This is a time when not enough rain and snow fall. When Mesopotamia experienced a drought, the level of the rivers fell. That made it hard for farmers to water their crops, which caused crops to fail. When crops failed, many people starved.

By about 6000 B.C., farmers in Mesopotamia set up canals to get water from the rivers to their fields. This system is called irrigation.

2. Why did Mesopotamian farmers set up irrigation systems?

_____

_____

Finding Resources

(pages 85–86)

How did Mesopotamians cope with a lack of resources?

Mesopotamia had no forests or stone and minerals. That meant that it had no wood and few building materials. As a result, Mesopotamians used mud to make bricks and plaster.

Mesopotamia was an easy place to invade. This is because it had few mountains or other barriers. As a result, people from other regions often invaded Mesopotamia. These people stole from the Mesopotamians or conquered them. To protect themselves, Mesopotamians built mud walls around their villages.

Mesopotamians traded grain for goods they needed, such as stone and wood. They were able to do this because they had a **surplus** of grain. This means that they had more grain than they needed for themselves.

3. How did Mesopotamians use their environment to make building materials?

_____

_____

_____

_____

READING STUDY GUIDE

CHAPTER 3 | LESSON 2 The First Civilization

Lesson 2 The First Civilization

BEFORE YOU READ

In Lesson 2, you will learn why the first civilization started in Mesopotamia.

AS YOU READ

Use a web diagram like this one to record the traits Sumer had that led to the start of the first civilization there.

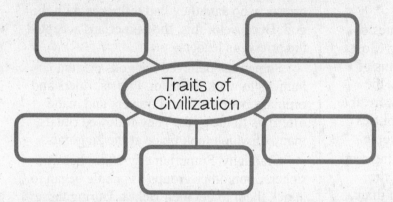

Traits of Civilization

TERMS & NAMES
- **civilization** an advanced form of culture
- **Sumer** a region in southern Mesopotamia and the site of the first civilization
- **city-state** a community that included a city and its nearby farmlands
- **ziggurat** the largest and most important structure in a Sumerian city
- **polytheism** a belief in many gods and goddesses
- **king** the highest-ranked leader of a group of people

The Rise of Civilization

(pages 89–91)

How did civilization develop in the region of Sumer?

After people began to farm, they did not have to search for food. Because of this, they were able to settle in villages. As more and more people settled in villages, the communities grew larger and in time became cities. Workers in these cities were organized to help solve problems. After a while, society and culture became more complex. This led to an advanced form of culture called **civilization.** The first civilization started in a region in the southern part of Mesopotamia around 3300 B.C. It was called **Sumer.**

Sumer had five traits that make a civilization.

- A civilization has advanced cities. Cities provide people with advantages. Sumerian cities provided people with temples in which to pray and different types of jobs.

- A civilization has workers that specialize. This means that the workers have jobs that require special skills, such as making

pottery. A society has to have a surplus of food to allow people to do other kinds of work besides farming. Also, people had to cooperate to work on projects. In Sumer, priests took on the job of organizing people to do such work.

- A civilization has institutions. An institution is a group of people who have a specific purpose. Religion and government became institutions.

- A civilization has a way of keeping records to keep track of things, such as food supplies. Keeping records often involves writing. The people of Mesopotamia invented the world's first system of writing.

- A civilization has advanced technology. Sumerians built canals to irrigate crops. They made tools of bronze.

1. Why is a surplus of food necessary to have specialized workers?

_____

_____

READING STUDY GUIDE

Sumerian City-States

(pages 91–92)

What new type of community developed in Sumer?

Sumerian cities were centers of trade, learning, and religion. At the time, most people still lived in the countryside. But eventually, cities began to rule the villages in the countryside. A community that included a city and its nearby lands was called a **city-state.** Each city-state ruled itself.

Some of the more famous city-states of Sumer included Kish, Nippur, and Ur. Most city-states were located near the mouths of the Tigris and Euphrates rivers, where the land was most fertile. Farmers there were able to produce food surpluses. These surpluses helped to feed a greater number of people.

Sumerian cities had narrow, winding roads. Walls built for protection surrounded the cities. Sumerian houses were made of thick, mud walls. Such walls helped to keep the heat out. A house was made up of a few rooms arranged around a courtyard.

The largest and most important building in a Sumerian city was the temple. It was called a **ziggurat.** The ziggurat was also the center of city life. Priests ran the irrigation systems at the ziggurat. People paid the priests for their services with grain. As a result, priests controlled the storage of surplus grain and much of the city-state's wealth.

2. Why did many Sumerian city-states develop near the mouth of the Tigris and Euphrates rivers?

_____

_____

_____

Changes in Leadership

(pages 93–95)

How did the leadership of Sumer change?

Sumerians believed in many gods and goddesses. This kind of belief is called **polytheism.** Sumerians believed in four main gods. They also had thousands of lesser gods.

The Sumerians believed the gods could prevent problems such as droughts. So people tried to please the gods. Each god had many priests, who said they had influence with the god. Because of this, the Sumerians accepted the priests as leaders.

Sumerians believed the gods created humans to work for them. Priests, rulers and ordinary people all said prayers and made offerings to the gods. They followed rituals, many of which took place at the ziggurats.

Gradually, Sumerian city-states became richer. Soon other groups of people began to attack them to get their riches. During these dangerous times, the people of the city-states chose a powerful leader to protect their city. At first, these leaders ruled only during wars. Later, they ruled full-time. The leaders took over the jobs of the priests. In time, this kind of leader became a **king.** This is the highest-ranked leader of a group of people. The land a king ruled was called a kingdom. Sumer was a kingdom by 2375 B.C. People believed that the gods let the kings rule.

3. Why did the people of Sumer choose a powerful leader?

_____

_____

_____

CHAPTER 3 | LESSON 3 Life in Sumer

Lesson 3 Life in Sumer

BEFORE YOU READ

In Lesson 3, you will learn about Sumerian society and culture.

AS YOU READ

Use this chart to take notes about the society, technology, and writing of Sumer.

Life in Sumer		
Society	Technology	Writing

TERMS & NAMES
- **bronze** a mixture of copper and tin
- **pictograph** picture writing
- **stylus** a sharpened reed used to make markings in clay
- **cuneiform** wedge-shaped writing
- **scribe** a person who specialized in writing

Sumerian Society

(pages 99–100)

What were the social classes that made up Sumerian society?

Sumerian society was divided into social groups, or classes. The kings and priests made up the top of the upper classes. Landowners, government officials, and wealthy merchants also made up the upper class.

All free people made up the in-between classes. Most Sumerians were in this class, including many farmers and artisans. Slaves made up the lowest class.

Most slaves in Sumer were taken as prisoners during wars. Children whose parents died or were very poor might become slaves who worked in the temple. A free person who owed more money than he or she could repay might become slaves. These people stayed slaves until they worked off their debt. Slaves had some rights and could also buy their freedom.

Women in Sumer had more rights than they did in later Mesopotamia. Some upper-class women became priestesses. Free women could own land or be merchants and artisans. But a woman's main role was to raise her children.

1. To what social class did most Sumerians belong?

_____

_____

_____

READING STUDY GUIDE

READING STUDY GUIDE CONTINUED

Sumerian Science and Technology

(pages 100–101)

What tools did the Sumerians invent?

Sumerians made several inventions to improve their lives. Some people believe that they invented the plow and the wheel. The plow helped Sumerian farmers break up soil, which made planting easier.

The Sumerians used the wheel in several ways. They used it on wagons to help move goods more easily. The wagons helped farmers take their crops to market more easily.

The potter's wheel helped Sumerians make pottery. Before the potter's wheel, people made pottery by shaping coils of clay by hand. The potter's wheel helped Sumerians make more pottery faster. The pots were important containers for surplus food.

Sumerians were one of the first people to use bronze. **Bronze** is a mixture of copper and tin. This metal was stronger than copper. Because of this, tools made from bronze lasted longer than copper tools. Bronze tools were one of the items Sumerians traded.

Sumerians used arithmetic to keep records of crops and trade goods. They had a number system that was based on the number 60. So today, we have 60 seconds in a minute and 60 minutes in an hour. Circles have 360 degrees. Sumerians used geometric shapes to make bricks, set up ramps, and dig canals.

2. How did Sumerians use arithmetic?

_____

_____

_____

Creation of Written Language

(pages 101–103)

How did the Sumerians invent writing?

Sumerians invented writing to help them in business. They needed to keep records of goods they traded. They also wanted to label goods.

At first, Sumerians used clay tokens that had a picture of the item to keep track of goods. They placed the tokens in containers and marked the containers so people would know what was inside them. The marks were a symbol of the item. These symbols are known as **pictographs,** which means "picture writing." Eventually, they stopped using tokens and used pictographs on clay tablets.

Early pictographs showed the actual objects. Later, they also showed ideas and sounds. In this way, Sumerians could write more words. Sumerians used a sharpened reed called a **stylus** to make wedge-shaped markings in a clay tablet. Eventually, they stopped using pictures and began to use symbols made of these wedge shapes. This kind of wedge-shaped writing is called **cuneiform.**

Sumerian writing was difficult to learn. As a result, few people were able to read and write. Those who specialized in writing were called **scribes.** They were professional record keepers. Scribes were very respected by the Sumerians.

Sumerians first used records for business. Later, they began keeping records of events, such as wars and floods. These records are the written history of Sumer. Other cultures in Mesopotamia also used the cuneiform writing system to keep records.

3. How did Sumerians use their writing system?

_____

_____

_____

CHAPTER 3 | Ancient Mesopotamia

Chapter 3 Ancient Mesopotamia

Glossary/After You Read

advanced beyond others in development or progress

current a flowing part of a river or stream

daily taking place every day

label to mark an object with a name or symbol that identifies it

mouth the part of a river that empties into a larger body of water

reed the hollow stem of a tall grass

swell to increase in size or volume

Terms & Names

A. Write the letter of the name or term that matches the description.

_____ **1.** a belief in many gods and goddesses

_____ **2.** having more than is needed for oneself

_____ **3.** a person who specialized in writing

_____ **4.** an advanced form of culture

_____ **5.** a period when not enough rain and snow fall

a. drought

b. surplus

c. civilization

d. polytheism

e. cuneiform

f. scribe

B. In the blank, write the letter of the choice that best completes the statement or answers the question.

_____ **6.** What kind of climate did Mesopotamia have?

    a. cold and wet   **b.** cold and dry   **c.** semiarid   **d.** humid

_____ **7.** The most important structure in a Sumerian city was the

    a. city-state.   **b.** ziggurat.   **c.** pictograph.   **d.** stylus.

_____ **8.** Sumerians were among the first people to make tools of

    a. bronze.   **b.** copper.   **c.** gold.   **d.** silver.

_____ **9.** Who made up the top of the upper classes of Sumer?

    a. landowners and wealthy merchants   **b.** the king and the priests   **c.** slaves   **d.** farmers

_____ **10.** What was the wedge-shaped writing used by the Sumerians called?

    a. pictograph   **b.** polytheism   **c.** stylus   **d.** cuneiform

READING STUDY GUIDE

READING STUDY GUIDE CONTINUED

Main Ideas

11. Why was Mesopotamia a good region for farming?

_____

_____

12. What five traits helped to make Sumer the world's first civilization?

_____

_____

13. Why did Sumerians try to please their gods and accept their priests as leaders?

_____

_____

14. How did the plow and the wheel help to improve the lives of Sumerians?

_____

_____

15. Why were scribes very respected by the Sumerians?

_____

_____

Thinking Critically

16. Summarizing How did Sumerians use or change their environment to improve their lives?

_____

_____

17. Forming and Supporting Opinions What do you think is the most important invention made by the Sumerians? Why do you think so?

_____

_____

READING STUDY GUIDE

CHAPTER 4 | LESSON 1 Mesopotamian Empires

Lesson 1 Mesopotamian Empires

BEFORE YOU READ

In this lesson, you will read about the first empires to develop in Mesopotamia.

AS YOU READ

Use this chart to make summarizing statements about each topic.

Topic	Statement
Geography	
A strong king	
A law code	

TERMS & NAMES

- **empire** Many different lands and people under one rule
- **emperor** The ruler of an empire
- **Fertile Crescent** An area of fertile, curved land along the eastern Mediterranean Sea
- **Hammurabi** A powerful Babylonian ruler who developed a single body of laws
- **code of law** A set of written rules
- **justice** Fair treatment

The First Empire Builders

(pages 113–114)

Who ruled Mesopotamia?

Between 3000 and 2000 B.C., kings of the city-states in Sumer fought. They wanted to gain more land. They wanted more wealth and power, too.

One of these kings was Sargon of Akkad. In about 2350 B.C. this *ambitious* ruler took over all of Mesopotamia. He brought many different peoples and lands under his control. This created the first **empire** in the world. It was called the Akkadian Empire.

In time, Sargon made himself **emperor** over lands from the Mediterranean Sea to the Persian Gulf. This area is called the **Fertile Crescent.** It has rich soil and plenty of water. Unlike the dry areas around it, the Fertile Crescent is good farmland.

The Akkadian Empire controlled many lands. This helped to spread ideas and ways of

life. One of the most important ideas was the Akkadian way of writing.

Empires were important in this way. They brought new ways of life to different places. They changed how people live. Sometimes they brought peace. They encouraged trade.

Sargon had started a *pattern* of empire making. What he did would be repeated. Over and over, new empires would rise and fall.

1. How did an empire like Sargon's affect the lives of the people in it?

_____

_____

_____

READING STUDY GUIDE

The Babylonian Empire

(page 114)

Which empires ruled the Fertile Crescent?

Sargon's empire lasted for about 200 years. Then outside attacks brought it down. City-states within the empire fought among themselves, too.

In about 2000 B.C. the Amorites invaded Mesopotamia. They took over all the city-states of Sumer. They made Babylon their capital city. It was on the Euphrates River. Their empire was called the Babylonian Empire, after their capital.

From 1792 to 1750 B.C. a powerful Amorite ruled the empire. His name was **Hammurabi.** He expanded the empire across Mesopotamia. He took over other parts of the Fertile Crescent, too.

Hammurabi had good ideas. He used *governors* to rule lands for him. He hired people to collect taxes. He appointed judges. Hammurabi also watched over farming, trade, and building.

2. What was the name of Hammurabi's empire?

_____

_____

_____

Hammurabi's Law Code

pages 115–116)

Why did Hammurabi create a law code?

The Babylonian Empire was large. It held many lands and different cultures. Each group had its own sets of laws. Hammurabi wanted one **code of law** for all his people. He thought that a written set of laws would help him rule better.

First, Hammurabi sent out people to collect all the existing sets of laws. Next, he studied the laws. Then, he put them together into one code of law. The code was written on huge pillars near a temple. There everyone could see the laws for themselves.

The laws were different for each social *class.* However, the new code brought some **justice** to the people. It gave people rights, too. It told everyone what punishments were given for which crimes.

Hammurabi's law code started an important idea. It made people think that government should protect them and give them justice. Before the code, people had taken their own revenge. Now, society was ruled by laws that everyone had to follow.

3. Why did Hammurabi post his law code on pillars?

_____

_____

_____

CHAPTER 4 | LESSON 2 Assyria Rules the Fertile Crescent

Lesson 2 Assyria Rules the Fertile Crescent

BEFORE YOU READ

In this lesson, you will read how people called the Assyrians built a large and powerful empire in Mesopotamia.

AS YOU READ

Use this chart to take notes about the effects of Assyrian rule.

Causes	Effects
Assyrian military machine	
Cruelty to captured peoples	
Huge empires	

TERMS & NAMES

- **exile** The forced removal of people from their homelands
- **tribute** Payment for protection
- **Hanging Gardens of Babylon** In ancient Babylon, an artificial mountain covered with gardens

A Mighty Military Machine

(pages 119–120)

How were the Assyrians able to build an empire?

Assyria was in northern Mesopotamia. Its rulers had to protect their lands. To do this, they built a powerful army. The Assyrians began to use their army to take over neighboring lands.

The Assyrian army was hard to beat. The soldiers fought fiercely. They battled on foot, on horseback, and in chariots. The Assyrians used the latest war technology, too. They had iron swords and iron-tipped spears. Few of their enemies had iron weapons. When attacking cities, the Assyrians used *battering rams,* ladders, and tunnels. In this way they could get past the gates and walls.

Once they got inside a city, they were cruel. If people surrendered they could choose a leader. If they refused, their own leaders were speared. The city was burned. Most of the rest of the people were killed or enslaved. Others were sent into **exile.** Because of all this, the Assyrians were greatly feared.

1. How did the Assyrians treat the peoples they conquered?

_____

_____

Assyria Builds a Huge Empire
(pages 120–121)

How did the Assyrians control their empire?

Between 850 and 650 B.C., the Assyrians built a huge empire. It included Syria, Babylon, Palestine, and Egypt. Under Ashurbanipal (668–627 B.C.) the empire reached its peak. It controlled almost all of the Fertile Crescent.

Because the empire was so big, it needed to be well organized. Like Hammurabi, the Assyrians chose governors or native kings to help them rule. The Assyrian army protected all the lands.

The rulers of the conquered lands also sent **tribute.** These payments brought money and goods into the empire's *treasury.* If a ruler did not pay tribute, the army came. It destroyed cities. The people were forced into exile.

The Assyrians made many enemies by their cruel acts. Exiled peoples tried to fight back. The Assyrians had to put down many revolts.

Two groups of enemies were the Medes and the Chaldeans. In 609 B.C. they worked together to defeat the hated Assyrians. They burned the capital city of Nineveh to ashes. The Assyrian Empire fell.

2. How did the Assyrians use the army to control the empire?

_____

_____

_____

A New Babylonian Empire
(pages 121–123)

What empire replaced the Assyrian Empire?

Soon the Chaldeans took over much of the old Assyrian Empire. They made Babylon their capital. The Chaldean Empire reached its peak between 605 and 562 B.C. At this time Nebuchadnezzar II was the emperor. He recaptured Syria. He conquered trading cities on the Mediterranean Sea, too.

Nebuchadnezzar also rebuilt Babylon. He constructed the huge, colorful Ishtar Gate. A giant ziggurat called the Tower of Babel *loomed* in the middle of the city. Astronomers climbed 300 feet to the top. There they studied the skies.

To please his wife, the emperor also built the **Hanging Gardens of Babylon.** This human-made mountain was covered with plants and trees. It was so amazing that it became one of the Seven Wonders of the World.

However, like the Assyrians, the Chaldeans had to deal with revolts. A group called the Hebrews rebelled in 598 B.C. Nebuchadnezzar took over their capital, Jerusalem. The Hebrews' temple was destroyed. The Chaldeans held thousands of Hebrews captive in Babylon for about 50 years.

Also, after Nebuchadnezzar the rulers were weak. There was conflict about religion in the empire, too. When Cyrus of Persia came, these problems made it easy for him to take over the Chaldean Empire.

3. Who were the Chaldeans?

_____

_____

_____

CHAPTER 4 | LESSON 3 Persia Controls Southwest Asia

Lesson 3 Persia Controls Southwest Asia

BEFORE YOU READ

In this lesson, you will read how people called the Persians created a huge empire across Southwest Asia.

AS YOU READ

Use this Venn diagram to take notes about the problems faced by the Persian rulers Cyrus and Darius.

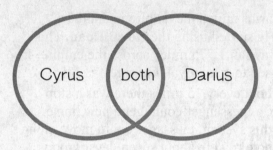

Cyrus both Darius

A Land Between East and West

(pages 129–130)

What was the land of the Persians like?

The Persians were nomads. They came from Central Asia. Around 1000 B.C. they settled on lands under the rule of the Medes. Modern-day Iran is on what used to be Persian land.

This land is varied. Mountain ranges keep it *isolated* from the sea and the rest of Southwest Asia. These ranges are the Zagros, Caucasus and the Hindu Kush. Most people lived at the edge of a high plateau. Others lived in mountain valleys. This area was rich in iron, copper, and *semiprecious* gems.

TERMS & NAMES

- **Anatolia** An area in Southwest Asia, also called Asia Minor, within modern-day Turkey
- **toleration** Allowing people to keep their customs and beliefs
- **province** An area of land similar to a state
- **satrap** A governor of a province in the Persian Empire
- **Royal Road** A 1,775-mile highway built across the Persian Empire for sending royal messages

---

After 1000 B.C., the Persians began to make their own tiny kingdoms. They got rich from trade. They traded in horses and minerals with peoples in eastern and western Asia. Their kingdoms grew and threatened the Medes rule.

1. Who were the Persians and where did they come from?

_____

_____

_____

READING STUDY GUIDE

READING STUDY GUIDE CONTINUED

Cyrus Founds the Persian Empire

(pages 130–131)

What was the rule of Cyrus like?

The Medes ruled the Persians until a king named Cyrus took control. Cyrus was a brilliant and powerful ruler. He was later called Cyrus the Great. This king had an idea. He wanted to conquer surrounding lands. His goal was to build a huge Persian empire.

To meet his goal, Cyrus made swift, attacks on nearby areas. First, he conquered **Anatolia,** or Asia Minor. Then he conquered the lands that once belonged to the Assyrians and Chaldeans. His empire was now very large.

Cyrus needed ways to rule his empire. It was filled with many different people. Cyrus did not want to rule like the Assyrians. Instead, he set up a *policy* of **toleration.** He let people keep their customs and ways of life. They could keep their religious beliefs, too. However, they did have to pay tribute.

Because of his wise rule, Cyrus made friends, not enemies. For example, he freed the Hebrews. He also let them rebuild their temple and the city of Jerusalem. For this he was very popular with the Hebrews. Acts like this made governing the empire easier for Cyrus. There were fewer revolts and more peace.

2. How did Cyrus's way of ruling help him to govern?

_____

_____

Darius Expands the Empire

(pages 132–133)

How did Darius control his empire?

The emperor after Cyrus was weak. Peoples in the empire started to rebel. However, the next ruler was strong, like Cyrus. His name was Darius.

Darius spent the first years of his rule putting down revolts. When this was done, he began conquering new lands. He pushed the

Persian Empire as far east as India. It was now 2,800 miles across.

The Persian Empire was so large that Darius had to think of new ways to rule. He divided the empire into 20 **provinces.** Each province had its own local government. A governor, called a **satrap,** ruled each province. The satraps collected taxes, too. Darius also sent out spies. These "king's eyes and ears" made sure that the satraps obeyed orders. In this way, Darius had good control over all his lands.

Darius united the empire in another way. He started using the **Royal Road.** This roadway ran 1,775 miles across the empire. It was used to send royal messages.

About every 15 miles there was a stop. There, a messenger could get a new horse. With this system, messages could move along the whole road in about seven days. Troops and mail could also move quickly around the empire. The road also encouraged trade.

Darius made other helpful changes, too. He set up a law code based on Hammurabi's. From his subjects, the Lydians, Darius copied the idea of minted coins. These coins could be used throughout the empire. They encourage business and made it easier to collect taxes.

In 486 B.C., Darius planned to march against Egyptian rebels. However, he died before he could go. Darius's son Xerxes then became the next ruler of the Persian Empire.

3. How did the idea of provinces help Darius control the empire?

_____

_____

Chapter 4 Early Empires

Glossary/After You Read

ambitious eager to gain success, fame, or power

battering ram a large, wooden beam used to knock down walls or gates during a siege

class a group of people having about the same social and economic standing

governor a person chosen to rule over a colony or territory

isolate to keep apart from others

loom to stand high over

pattern a series of repeated events

policy a course of action chosen by a government

semiprecious less valuable than the most expensive

treasury the place where a government keeps its money

wise showing intelligence and good judgment

wonder a very unusual or remarkable thing

Terms & Names

A. Read each sentence. Then write the letter of the word that could best replace the underlined part.

a. code of law   c. satrap   e. empire   g. exile

b. toleration   d. justice   f. tribute

_____ **1.** As a <u>governor of a province</u> under Darius, the man had to collect taxes.

_____ **2.** Cyrus had a policy of <u>allowing people to keep their own customs and beliefs</u>.

_____ **3.** Conquered rulers had to send the Assyrians <u>payments in money and goods</u> to keep from being destroyed.

_____ **4.** Hammurabi created <u>a written set of laws</u> to help rule his lands.

_____ **5.** The Assyrians would punish people with <u>sending them away from their homeland</u>.

_____ **6.** Sargon built the first <u>collection of many peoples and lands under one ruler in the world</u>.

B. Write the letter of the name or term that best matches the description.

_____ **7.** The Babylonian emperor who made changes to the law

_____ **8.** A highway for sending messages in the Persian Empire

_____ **9.** A curve-shaped area of rich soil in Southwest Asia

_____ **10.** One of the Seven Wonders of the World

a. Hanging Gardens of Babylon

b. Hammurabi

c. Royal Road

d. Anatolia

e. Fertile Crescent

READING STUDY GUIDE CONTINUED

Main Ideas

11. What was special about Sargon's Akkadian Empire?

_____

_____

12. What was the purpose of Hammurabi's code?

_____

13. How did the Assyrians build and control their empire?

_____

_____

14. How was Cyrus' rule different from earlier empires?

_____

_____

15. What was important about the location of the Persian Empire?

_____

_____

Thinking Critically

16. Making Generalizations What were some difficulties faced by rulers of all the early empires?

_____

_____

_____

17. Making Inferences Think about the Chaldean and Persian Empires. Why was it important that the emperor be a strong leader?

_____

_____

_____

READING STUDY GUIDE

CHAPTER 5 | LESSON 1 Gift of the Nile

Lesson 1 Gift of the Nile

BEFORE YOU READ

In this lesson, you will learn how the Nile River in Egypt helped people create a civilization.

AS YOU READ

Use this chart to take notes about why Egyptian civilization developed along the Nile River. Answering the question at the end of each section will help you fill in the chart.

Causes	Effects
Floods	
New agricultural techniques	
Many land resources	

TERMS & NAMES

- **cataract** waterfall
- **delta** area near a river's mouth where the water deposits fine soil
- **silt** fine soil deposited by a river
- **fertile** good for growing crops
- **linen** type of fabric woven from flax plants

Geography of Ancient Egypt

(pages 147–148)

Why was the Nile River important?

A historian once called Egypt "the gift of the Nile" because the river made it possible for people to develop a civilization there.

The Nile is the longest river in the world. It flows north through Africa and ends in the Mediterranean Sea. It has many **cataracts** along the way. The cataracts end in southern Egypt, and the river is calm the rest of the way. Near the sea, the river splits into many streams and forms a **delta.** The water deposits **silt** in the delta.

Every summer, heavy rains fell in the south, and the Nile would flood. The rushing current would carry **fertile** black soil with it. The river flooded the land along the shores. As the water slowed, it set down the soil. The river flooded at the same time every year, so farmers knew when the land would be good for planting.

The ancient Egyptians lived in the black land where the river had put down the fertile soil. The land away from the river was a dry desert they called the red land. In Egypt, the weather was always sunny. For eight months it was hot. For the four months of winter, it was cooler.

The harsh desert stopped enemies from reaching Egypt. The Mediterranean coast was swampy and did not have good harbors. Since travel was hard, the early Egyptians did not travel far from home.

1. How did the Nile floods help farmers grow crops?

_____

_____

_____

Land of Plenty

(pages 148–149)

How did the Egyptians use the land around the Nile?

Egyptian farmers invented farming methods that gave them more farmland. They dug ditches that took river water to dry areas. Then they used a bucket on a pole to spread the water on the fields. They were using these methods by 2400 B.C.

Farmers grew many different foods. They grew vegetables, such as lettuce, radishes, asparagus, and cucumbers. They grew fruits, such as dates, figs, grapes, and watermelons. They grew wheat and made bread from it.

Egyptians made clothing from plants. Thread made from the flax plant was woven into a cloth called **linen.** Linen is light and cool. Men wore wraps around their waists. Women wore loose, sleeveless dresses. Egyptians used the reeds that grew in marshes to make sandals. Reeds are tall grasses.

Egyptian houses were made of bricks. The roofs were made of sticks and palm trees. Houses had high windows to keep out the sunlight. They were often painted white to reflect away the heat. Woven reed mats covered the dirt floors. Most people slept on mats with linen sheets. Rich people had beds and cushions.

Nobles had fancy homes with courtyards with shade trees. Some had pools filled with lotus flowers and fish. Poorer people went to the roof to cool off after sunset. They often cooked, ate, and slept outside.

2. How did new farming methods help Egyptians grow all of the food they needed?

_____

_____

_____

Geography Shapes Egyptian Life

(pages 150–151)

What economic activities developed in Egypt?

Egypt's economy was based on farming. But people did many other jobs too.

Mining was important work. Egyptians used copper to make tools and weapons. They knew how to use copper as early as 6000 B.C. Later they learned that iron was stronger and began to use that. They also mined gold to make jewelry and special objects. Nubia, in the south, had the richest gold mines.

Mining was hot and difficult work. Copper and iron were found in the mountains of the Sinai Peninsula. This desert lies east of Egypt.

The Egyptians also mined precious stones. They used precious stones to make jewelry. Turquoise was a kind of precious stone that came from the Sinai.

Egyptians fished for and hunted the animals that lived along the river. People made rafts out of reeds to go on the river. They used nets and harpoons to catch fish. Spears were used to hunt hippopotamuses and crocodiles. Small birds, such as quail, were caught with nets. People also hunted ducks and geese.

Over time, the Egyptians began to use the Nile for travel. They added sails and oars to their boats. They did not always need to row their boats. The river current flowed north, so boats could drift when going toward the delta. However, the winds blew toward the south. Travelers could raise their sails to go in that direction.

Because the Nile provided so much, Egyptians had extra products they could trade. They did not have money, so they exchanged goods. This type of trade is called barter.

3. How did Egyptians use the natural resources they had?

_____

_____

CHAPTER 5 | LESSON 2 Life in Ancient Egypt

Lesson 2 Life in Ancient Egypt

BEFORE YOU READ

In the last lesson, you read how Egyptians prospered along the Nile. In this lesson you will read about how this prosperity made life easier and provided greater opportunities for many Egyptians.

AS YOU READ

Use this web diagram to understand aspects of Egyptian culture.

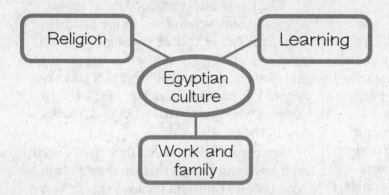

TERMS & NAMES
- **scribe** a person whose job was to write and keep records
- **hieroglyph** a picture that stands for different words or sounds
- **papyrus** paperlike material
- **afterlife** a life believed to follow death
- **embalm** to preserve a body after death
- **mummy** a body that has been dried so it won't decay

Work and Family Life

(pages 155–157)

How did work and social roles affect people in ancient Egypt?

As farmers grew more food than they could eat themselves, the society's economy began to grow. In time, many people were able to turn from farming to other types of work. Egyptian society became more complex. It had many levels. At the top of Egyptian society was the ruler. The king had the greatest power in Egyptian society. Next came priests and nobles. Priests carried out ceremonies and took care of the temples. Priests and rulers held ceremonies to please the gods. Egyptians believed that if the gods were angry, the Nile would not flood and crops would not grow.

Just below the priests and nobles were government officials and **scribes.** Egypt's leaders divided the country into 42 provinces.

In each province, government officials kept the provinces running smoothly. Scribes were people whose job was to write and keep records. Next came craftspeople and merchants. Some craftspeople built stone or brick houses and temples. Others made pottery, furniture, clothing, sandals, jewelry, or other goods. Merchants sold goods, and traders traveled to the upper Nile to trade with other Africans. They exchanged Egyptian goods for animal skins, live beasts, and exotic woods.

Slaves were at the bottom of society. In Egypt, people became slaves if they owed a debt, committed a crime, or were captured in war. Most Egyptian slaves were treated well and usually freed after a period of time. Slaves who worked in the mines had a much harder life. Many died from overwork.

In Egyptian society, men and women had fairly equal rights. They could both own and manage their own property. The main job of most women was to care for their children and home. Some also wove cloth or worked with their husbands in fields or workshops. Some even rose to key positions in the government.

1. What groups were at the top and at the bottom of Egyptian society?

_____

_____

Expanding Knowledge

(pages 157–158)

How did learning advance in ancient Egypt?

Egyptian priests studied the sky as part of their religion. They created the world's first practical calendar. The Egyptians also developed early geometry. They developed practical ways to measure the land. Architects used geometric shapes such as squares and triangles to design temples and monuments. Egyptian doctors learned about the human body by preparing the dead for burial. That knowledge helped them perform some of the world's first surgery. Around 3000 B.C., Egyptians developed a writing system using **hieroglyphs.** Hieroglyphs are pictures that stand for different words or sounds. They also made a form of paper from a plant known as **papyrus.** Papyrus scrolls were light and easy to carry. Egyptians used them to create some of the first books.

2. What advances in learning did the Egyptians make?

_____

_____

_____

Beliefs and Religion

(pages 159–161)

What religious beliefs did Egyptians hold?

The Egyptians had a positive view of life. Their fertile soil allowed them to meet most of their needs. They did not have to struggle to make a living. Their positive outlook shaped their religion. It led them to believe that the gods favored them. Egyptians believed that they would have a happy and prosperous **afterlife.** An afterlife is a life believed to follow death.

The Egyptians worshiped many gods. Many of them were related to the afterlife or to nature. The Egyptians worshiped the sun, river, and plant gods. Important Egyptian gods included Re, the sun god; Osiris, a god who judged Egyptians after death; Isis, a fertility goddess who was Osiris' wife; and Anubis, god of the dead.

Egyptians believed that they would need their bodies in the afterlife, so they embalmed dead people. **Embalm** means to preserve a body after death. Embalmers removed all organs except the heart and filled the body with a mixture of salt and herbs to create a **mummy.** A mummy is a body that has been dried so it won't decay. When dry, the mummy was wrapped in hundred of yards of linen strips. It was placed inside a coffin inside a tomb. The tomb also held furniture, food, and other everyday objects the dead would need for the afterlife.

3. What did the Egyptians think happened after death?

_____

_____

CHAPTER 5 | LESSON 3 The Pyramid Builders

Lesson 3 The Pyramid Builders

BEFORE YOU READ

In this lesson you will read about the rulers who governed Egypt during the periods of history known as the Old Kingdom and Middle Kingdom.

AS YOU READ

As you read Lesson 3, use the diagram below to summarize the main ideas and important details of this lesson.

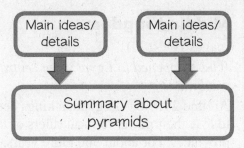

Main ideas/details → Main ideas/details → Summary about pyramids

TERMS & NAMES

- **dynasty** a line of rulers from the same family
- **succession** the order in which members of a royal family inherit a throne
- **pharaoh** a king of Egypt, the name meant "great house"
- **pyramid** a structure shaped like a triangle with four sides that meet at a point
- **step pyramid** a pyramid whose sides rise in a series of giant steps
- **Khufu** pharaoh who built the largest pyramid ever constructed

The Old Kingdom

(pages 165–166)

What kind of government ruled Egypt after it was united?

According to legend, a king named Narmer united Upper and Lower Egypt. Narmer may represent several kings who slowly joined the two lands under one central government. After that, Egypt remained a united country with a strong central government for thousands of years. The country was ruled by a series of dynasties. A **dynasty** is a line of rulers from the same family. More than 30 dynasties ruled ancient Egypt. When a king died, one of his children usually took his place as ruler. The order in which members of a royal family inherit a throne is called the **succession.**

Historians divide ancient Egyptian history into three periods: the Old Kingdom, the Middle Kingdom, and the New Kingdom. The Old Kingdom started about 2575 B.C., when the Egyptian empire was getting stronger.

The king of Egypt became known as the **pharaoh.** The pharaoh ruled from the capital city of Memphis. The ancient Egyptians thought the pharaoh was a god. They believed that if the pharaoh and his subjects honored the gods, their lives would be happy. If Egypt had hard times, the people blamed the pharaoh for angering the gods. Then another leader might drive him from power and start a new dynasty. Because the pharaoh was thought to be a god, government and religion were not separate. Priests had much power in the government. Many high officials were priests.

1. How were religion and government linked in ancient Egypt?

_____

_____

READING STUDY GUIDE CONTINUED

Khufu's Great Pyramid

(pages 166–169)

How did Pharaoh Khufu proclaim his glory?
The first rulers of Egypt were often buried in an underground tomb topped by mud brick. Later kings wanted more permanent monuments. They built small brick or stone pyramids over their tombs. A **pyramid** is a structure shaped like a triangle with four sides that meet at a point. About 2630 B.C., King Djoser built a much larger pyramid called a **step pyramid** over his tomb. A step pyramid has sides that rise in a series of giant steps.

About 80 years later, a pharaoh named **Khufu** ordered workers to construct the largest pyramid ever built. It was made from 2.3 million blocks of stone. He wanted a monument that would show the world how great he was. Building the pyramid was hard work. Farmers did the heavy labor of hauling stones during the season when the Nile flooded their fields. Skilled stonecutters and overseers worked year round. The Great Pyramid took nearly 20 years to build. About 20,000 Egyptians worked on it.

In time, Egyptians stopped building pyramids because the pyramids attracted robbers. Grave robbers broke into the tombs to steal the treasures buried with the pharaohs. Sometimes they also stole the mummies. Egyptians believed that if a tomb was robbed, the person buried there could not have a happy afterlife. During the New Kingdom, pharaohs built more secret tombs in the Valley of the Kings. They hoped to protect their bodies and treasures from robbers. Although pharaohs tried hard to hide their tombs, robbers stole treasures from almost every tomb. Only one tomb built for a New Kingdom pharaoh was ever found with much of its treasure untouched.

Tombs were supposed to be the palaces of pharaohs in the afterlife. Mourners filled royal tombs with food, furniture, and other objects the pharaoh would need for the afterlife. Tomb walls were decorated with paintings and sculpture. The paintings showed pharaohs enjoying themselves in the afterlife.

2. Why did Khufu build such a large pyramid?

_____

_____

Middle Kingdom

(pages 169–170)

What happened to Egypt when centralized rule weakened?
Around 2130 B.C., Egyptian kings began to lose their power to local rulers of the provinces. For about 500 more years, the kings held Egypt together but with a much weaker central government. This period of Egyptian history is called the Middle Kingdom.

During this time, a nomadic people called the Hyksos invaded Egypt. They succeeded in conquering Egypt because they had better weapons and horse-drawn chariots. After about 100 years, the Egyptians drove out the Hyksos. and the New Kingdom began.

3. How was the Middle Kingdom different from the Old Kingdom?

_____

_____

READING STUDY GUIDE

Name   Period   Date

CHAPTER 5 | LESSON 4 The New Kingdom

Lesson 4 The New Kingdom

BEFORE YOU READ

In the last lesson you read about the Old and Middle Kingdom. In this lesson, you will read about some important rulers of the New Kingdom.

AS YOU READ

As you read Lesson 4, use the time line below to list the events that took place during the reigns of the pharaohs discussed in this lesson.

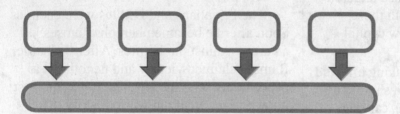

TERMS & NAMES

- **Hatshepsut** the first woman to rule as pharaoh
- **obelisk** type of monument with a four-sided shaft with a pyramid-shaped top
- **Ramses II** Egyptian pharaoh who took the throne in 1279 B.C., ruled for 66 years, and greatly expanded the empire by military means

A Woman Pharaoh

(pages 173–174)

What was the significance of Queen Hatshepsut's rule?

The New Kingdom included some of Egypt's most powerful rulers. These pharaohs moved the capital from Memphis to Thebes. They made Egypt stronger through trade and military conquest.

Queen **Hatshepsut** was the first woman to rule as pharaoh. She was the wife of a pharaoh who died soon after he took power. She then ruled with her stepson, Thutmose III. In 1472 B.C. she declared herself the only ruler. Unlike other New Kingdom pharaohs, Hatshepsut not only expanded Egypt by waging war, but also by increasing trade. She sent her largest trading expeditions across the eastern desert to the Red Sea. Egyptian ships sailed south to the African land of Punt. Traders returned with herbs, spices, live monkeys, and other rare and exotic goods.

Like other pharaohs, Hatshepsut built monuments to proclaim her glory. She had tall **obelisks** constructed on which carvers recorded her great deeds in hieroglyphs. An obelisk is a four-sided shaft with a pyramid-shaped top.

After ruling for 15 years, Hatshepsut disappeared. She may have died peacefully, or her stepson Thutmose III may have killed her. After her death, Thutmose became pharaoh and tried to destroy all record of her reign. We know about her today because her damaged temple and tomb were found and restored.

1. How did Hatshepsut try to make Egypt richer?

_____

_____

READING STUDY GUIDE CONTINUED

A Reforming Pharaoh

(pages 174–175)

How did Akhenaton try to change Egyptian religion?

Akhenaton became pharaoh in 1353 B.C. As ruler, he tried to change Egyptian religion. He declared a sun god named Aton the most important god and closed the temples of other gods. He promoted the worship of one god for the first time in Egyptian history.

Priests who served others gods suddenly lost power. They became angry. They also feared that the pharaoh's actions had angered the old gods. To avoid conflict with those priests, Akhenaton moved to a new capital called Akhetaton.

Akhenaton's new ways of thinking affected art. For the first time, Egyptian art showed a pharaoh realistically. For example, carvings of Akhenaton showed his large stomach.

Akhenaton's new religion did not last long. Three years after Akhenaton died, a young relative named Tutankhamen became pharaoh. The boy relied on his advisers to help him rule Egypt. They convinced him to reject the new religion and worship the old gods.

2. What changes did Akhenaton make?

_____

_____

_____

A Powerful Pharaoh

(pages 175–177)

How did Ramses II expand Egypt?

In 1279 B.C., 44 years after Tutankhamen died, **Ramses II** became pharaoh. His 66-year reign was among the longest in history. He was a strong military leader who expanded the empire through war. Under Ramses' rule, Egypt extended its territory south into the African kingdom of Nubia. The empire also stretched to the eastern rim of the Mediterranean Sea on the border with the Hittite empire.

The Egyptians and Hittites were enemies. Soon after he became pharaoh, Ramses led an army against the Hittites. After the battle, Ramses claimed victory and negotiated a peace treaty with the Hittites. It was the first known peace treaty in world history. After this treaty, no enemy threatened Egypt while Ramses ruled.

To honor himself, Ramses built a city called the House of Ramses. It included a temple guarded by four 66-foot statues of Ramses himself. Ramses' long and peaceful reign made the Egyptian government stable. No enemy threatened Egypt while Ramses ruled.

After Ramses died, the central government slowly weakened. After about 1070 B.C., a series of foreign powers ruled Egypt. Alexander the Great, the king of Macedonia, conquered Egypt. After his death, Macedonians ruled Egypt for a long time. The last Macedonian ruler was Queen Cleopatra. In time, the Roman Empire conquered Egypt.

3. What were Ramses II's accomplishments?

_____

_____

_____

READING STUDY GUIDE

Chapter 5 Ancient Egypt

Glossary/After You Read

barren lacking plants or crops

noble a member of a wealthy and powerful family

formal carried out in a ceremonial manner

inherit to receive something from a person who has died

triangle a shape with three sides

reserved to keep for a special use

reign the time when a ruler is in power

status a position, rank, or standing give to someone or something

Terms & Names

A. Circle the name or term that best completes each sentence.

1. The area near the mouth of the Nile was a _____.

    delta   cataract   desert

2. Egyptians made _____ cloth out of the fibers of flax plants.

    linen   cotton   gold

3. A _____ was a person who wrote and kept records.

    scribe   mummy   slave

4. To preserve a body after death, Egyptians would _____ it.

    embalm   barter   worship

5. Some Egyptian pharaohs built _____ in honor of themselves.

    obelisks   shadufs   garments

B. Write the letter of the name of the pharaoh that matches the description.

_____ 6. Promoted the worship of only one god

_____ 7. Reigned for 66 years

_____ 8. Tried to destroy records about his stepmother

_____ 9. Made an important trip to Punt

_____ 10. Built a famous step pyramid

_____ 11. Built a pyramid that took 20 years to build

a. Hatshepsut

b. Thutmose III

c. Ramses II

d. Akhenaton

e. Djoser

f. Khufu

READING STUDY GUIDE

Main Ideas

12. How did the Nile River help farmers?

_____

_____

13. How are hieroglyphs different from modern English letters?

_____

_____

14. Why did Egyptians include everyday items in tombs?

_____

_____

15. What type of afterlife did Egyptians expect?

_____

_____

16. How did the desert help Egypt?

_____

_____

Thinking Critically

17. Making Inferences What do the pyramids show about ancient Egypt?

_____

_____

_____

18. Forming and Supporting Opinions Explain whether you think you would have liked to live in ancient Egypt.

_____

_____

Lesson 1 Nubia and the Land of Kush

BEFORE YOU READ

In this lesson, you will read about the ancient African kingdom of Kush.

AS YOU READ

Use this graphic organizer to order the events that happened in the kingdom of Kush.

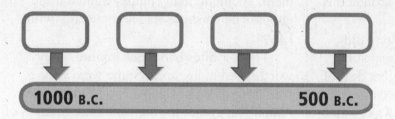

| 1000 B.C. | 500 B.C. |

TERMS & NAMES

- **Nubia** A geographic region of Africa, between Egypt and the sixth cataract of the Nile River
- **Kush** A kingdom in Nubia
- **Piankhi** A Kushite king who took over Egypt
- **Meroë** The capital of Kush during its second period
- **smelting** The heating of ore to separate the elements it contains

The Region of Nubia

(page 189)

How were Nubia and Egypt connected?

Nubia is a region in Africa. It started at the southern *boundary* of Egypt. It ended south of the Nile River's sixth cataract.

Like Egypt, Nubia was divided into two parts: upper and lower. These parts were based on their location along the Nile. Like the Egyptians, the people of Nubia lived along the Nile. However, in southern Nubia the climate was wetter. This made the land there good for farming. So in that area, people did not have to farm only along the Nile.

1. How was Nubia like and different from Egypt?

_____

_____

_____

The Kush Civilization

(pages 190–192)

What were some of the achievements of Piankhi?

Between 2000 and 1000 B.C. Egypt controlled Nubia. Nubia was a source of goods for the Egyptians. However, Egypt began to lose power. Then a Nubian kingdom called **Kush** took over.

In ancient times, Egypt borrowed ideas from Nubia. For example, some scholars think that Nubia had the first king. Later, this idea grew and changed in Egypt. The king became the pharaoh.

When Egypt took over Nubia, the pharaoh sent an *official* to govern there. Then the two cultures shared ideas and ways of life. Nubian peoples, such as those in Kush, used Egyptian ideas in art and architecture. For example, they built pyramids. They also worshiped some Egyptian gods.

Young Kushite nobles went to live in Egypt. They learned Egyptian. They wore Egyptian clothing and followed Egyptian customs. They brought back customs and royal rituals to Kush. They brought back the Egyptian system of writing, too.

READING STUDY GUIDE

In the 700s B.C., the kingdom of Kush began to take over Egypt. In 751 B.C., a Kushite king named **Piankhi** finished the conquest. He united Egypt and Kush. Piankhi became pharaoh. He was the first ruler of Egypt's 25th dynasty. Although he was Egypt's ruler, Piankhi lived in the capital of Kush. This was the city of Napata.

Napata was at the spot where an important road began. This road was used to move goods around the Nile's cataracts. Traders used the road when they could not *navigate* around this rough part of the river.

Nubia was rich in goods that Egypt did not have. These included ivory, animal skins, wood, and minerals. This led to a great deal of trade along the Nile. Napata also became the center of trade between Egypt and Kush's other trading partners.

In 671 B.C., the Assyrians invaded Egypt. The Kushite ruler at the time was Taharqa. He spent most of his rule fighting the Assyrians. However, the Assyrians had iron weapons. They had men who fought on horseback, or a cavalry. The Egyptians had only bronze weapons and no cavalry. The Assyrians eventually conquered all of Egypt and some of Kush. The Kushite kings retreated to the south.

2. What were some features of Kush's rule over Egypt?

_____

_____

The Kushite Capital of Meroë

(pages 192–193)

Why was the Kushite city of Meroë an important economic center?

The Kushite kings chose a new capital in 590 B.C. It was called **Meroë.** This city was on the Nile. It was also on trade routes between the Red Sea and inland Africa. It had access to gold and iron, too.

The wars with the Assyrians showed the Kushites that they needed iron weapons. So they learned about **smelting.** In this way they could get the iron they needed from the ore they *mined.*

Meroë was in an excellent place for making iron. It was near iron deposits. The Kushite built furnaces for smelting. They made their weapons. They also traded their iron around Africa in Arabia. The Kushites also traded in ivory and gold and items made from them. People in many places wanted these goods. The Kushites traded especially with Egypt.

The Kushites had a rich culture. They worshipped many gods. Some were very similar to those of Egypt. Two of these were Amon-Re, god of the sun, and Isis, goddess of the moon. Other gods were Nubian.

In Nubia, royal women played an important role. Queen Amanitore ruled with her husband around 23 B.C.

The people of Kush developed their own written language. It was first based on hieroglyphics. Later, it developed into an alphabet with 23 characters. No one has been able to read it yet.

Kushite royal tombs followed many Egyptian ideas. Kushite royals were buried in pyramids with flat tops. A chapel might be attached to the side. Kushite kings were often mummified. These customs continued in Nubia even after they had died out in Egypt.

3. How did Meroë's geography make it an important city?

_____

_____

READING STUDY GUIDE

Lesson 2 The Kingdom of Aksum

BEFORE YOU READ

In this lesson, you will read how a new and powerful kingdom arose in Africa.

AS YOU READ

Use this diagram to record the main ideas and details about Aksum.

1. _____
2. _____

The Kingdom of Aksum

1. _____
2. _____

1. _____
2. _____

TERMS & NAMES

- **Aksum** An ancient African kingdom in present-day Ethiopia and Eritrea
- **Horn of Africa** An area in eastern Africa shaped like the horn of a rhinoceros
- **Adulis** The main trading port of Aksum
- **Ezana** The first Christian king of Aksum
- **terrace** An area of land leveled for farming

The Rise of Aksum

(pages 197–198)

Why did trade become important to Aksum?

The kingdom of Kush was destroyed by a new power. This was **Aksum.** Aksum was located in what are Ethiopia and Eritrea today.

Aksum had a proud history. A *legend* tells that the dynasty of Aksum started with Menelik. He was the son of King Solomon of Israel and the Queen of Sheba.

Aksum was located on the **Horn of Africa.** Being located here gave Aksum access to many trade routes. It could trade with people on the Red Sea, Mediterranean Sea, Indian Ocean, and on the Nile River.

Like Kush, Aksum became a major trading hub and meeting place. Trade goods came to this area from Arabia, Persia, India, and other parts of Africa.

The main trading port of Aksum was **Adulis.** It was on the Red Sea. There, people traded many kinds of goods. These included salt, ivory, cloth, brass, iron, gold, glass, olive oil, and wine. Animal traders bought and sold animals such as giraffes and elephants.

1. What made Aksum a trading hub?

_____

_____

_____

King Ezana Expands Aksum

(page 198)

What was the effect of King Ezana on religion?

Aksum started out small. However, a strong king rose to power in A.D. 325. His name was **Ezana.** He greatly expanded Aksum's lands. He took over an Arab trading colony on the Arabian Peninsula. Then in 350, he conquered Kush. He burned Meroë to the ground.

At this time Aksum also expanded inland. It took over lands along the Red Sea. This put Aksum in control of a large trade *network.*

Ezana had become king when he was still an *infant.* His mother ruled for him until he was of age. One of his teachers taught the boy king about Christianity. When Ezana began to really rule, he became a Christian. He also made Christianity the official religion of Aksum. The Christian church in Aksum was linked to Alexandria, in Egypt, rather than to Rome.

2. What change did Ezana make to life in Aksum?

_____

_____

_____

_____

Aksum's Achievements

(pages 199–200)

What were some of Aksum's achievements?

Aksum developed a *unique* culture. It was based on a blending of ways of life on the Horn of Africa and in southern Arabia.

The pillars of Aksum were one of its achievements. These huge columns were from 60 to 100 feet tall. They were made without mortar and carved from one slab of stone. They had false doors and windows. They were placed around the country. Their purpose was to celebrate great victories or achievements. Builders in Kush and Egypt had used pillars much the same way.

Builders in Aksum also created large temples. Later, these were replaced with richly decorated Christian churches.

Aksum also had a written language. It was called Ge'ez. Arabs had brought it to Aksum. It became the basis for three languages spoken in the area today—Amharic, Tigrinya, and Tigre. Ge'ez is still used in the Ethiopian Church.

Aksum farmers also figured out a way to farm on the rugged land. They built **terraces.** They could farm more land on these flat areas. Aksum farmers also built canals, dams, and holding ponds to irrigate their fields.

3. What were the pillars of Aksum like?

_____

_____

_____

READING STUDY GUIDE

Lesson 3 West, Central, and Southern Africa

BEFORE YOU READ

In this lesson, you will read about the early peoples of west, central, and southern Africa.

AS YOU READ

Use this diagram to take notes about the movements of early peoples in Africa.

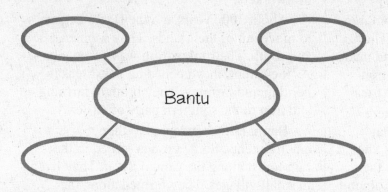

> **TERMS & NAMES**
> - **animism** The belief that everything has a soul
> - **griot** African storytellers and oral historians
> - **Nok** Early West African people who worked with iron
> - **Bantu** Several peoples who spoke similar languages and who spread throughout southern Africa
> - **migration** A move from one region to another

Early Life in Africa

(pages 203–205)

What were some of the environments that the people of west, central, and southern Africa had to adapt to?

The Sahara dried up around 4000 B.C. At that time people moved into West Africa. They went to the area around the Niger River. West, central, and southern Africa was mostly covered with savannas and rain forests.

The rain forests were not good for farming. Most people lived on savannas. These flat, grassy areas covered 40 percent of Africa. There, dry seasons *alternate* with rainy ones. Most people went to live here. They lived in small groups of several families.

However, the soil on savannas was not good for farming. This was mainly because the climate changed. Decertification also added to the problem. Most people lived by *herding*. They kept cattle, goats, and sheep.

Some practiced slash-and-burn farming. After a few years the soil became poor. Then

people had to move. Scholars think this kind of farming began in African around 6000 B.C.

Ancient Africans believed in many gods. However, they held one creator god higher than the others. They also believed that all things in nature have a soul. This belief is called **animism.**

These early peoples did not have written languages. However, they kept their history by telling stories. In some places there were special storytellers. They were called **griots.** It was the griot's job to recall old stories and create new ones. In that way, past events were remembered.

1. How did people adapt to life on the savannas?

_____

_____

_____

The Nok Culture

(page 205)

What role did ironworking play in Nok culture?

Many early peoples in Africa made things out of materials that did not last. For example, they might have made baskets out of plant fibers. Few objects from this time and area survived.

However, scientists did find artifacts from one culture. Between the Benue and Niger rivers scientists found small clay statues. They also found tools and materials from iron making. The scientists were surprised. They did not think that anyone in this area had made iron before 500 B.C. They also thought iron making had only happened in eastern Africa.

One of the groups who made iron here were the **Nok.** They lived in what is today southeast Nigeria. Unlike most peoples, the Nok did not first make copper. Instead, they went right into making iron. They were among the first *ironsmiths* in western Africa.

The Nok mined iron ore. They smelted the iron. They worked the iron into tools and weapons. Some of these items were traded across West Africa.

2. What did the Nok use iron for?

_____

_____

The Bantu Migrations

(pages 206–207)

Where did the Bantu peoples first live, and where did they move to?

The **Bantu** peoples lived in the same area as the Nok. The word *Bantu* means "the people." However, the Bantu were not one group. They were many groups. These groups had similar cultures and spoke similar languages. They were herders and farmers. Later they were ironworkers.

About 3000 years ago the Bantu began to move out of their lands. They went east and south. Their **migration** was a slow one. As they went, they opened up new areas to herding and farming. They brought farming and iron to the southern parts of Africa.

Bantu farmers adapted to their environments. Some groups settled in the rain forest along the Congo River. They lived in small villages. They farmed along the riverbanks. Other Bantu kept going south. They went to live on the grasslands of southern Africa. They began to raise animals and grow crops.

The Bantu changed things for the people who already lived on the land. In turn, the Bantu learned new ways. The Bantu learned cattle herding from people near present-day Lake Victoria. They forced hunter-gatherers out of their territories. The Bantu *intermarried* with other peoples. They shared their knowledge of iron making. They also shared ways of farming. As the Bantu spread, their languages spread, too.

3. What was the effect of the Bantu migrations?

_____

_____

CHAPTER 6 | Kush and Other African Kingdoms

Chapter 6 Kush and Other African Kingdoms

Glossary/After You Read

alternate to happen in turns, first one and then the other

boundary a border or line where something ends

herd to tend or watch over sheep, cattle, or other grazing animals

infant a child in the earliest stage of life

intermarried married to a member of another group

ironsmith a person who makes things out of iron

legend a story handed down from earlier times

mine to gather rocks or minerals from below ground

navigate to guide the course of a ship or aircraft

network a connected system, such as crisscrossing routes

official someone who holds a position of authority

unique one of a kind

Terms & Names

A. If the statement is true, write "true" on the line. If it is false, change the underlined words to make it true.

_____ **1.** The belief that all things have a soul is called <u>animation</u>.

_____ **2.** Iron is removed from ore in a process called <u>smelting</u>.

_____ **3.** A <u>griot</u> told stories to help remember past events.

_____ **4.** A move from one region to another is called <u>irrigation</u>.

_____ **5.** The city of <u>Meroë</u> was the main trading port of Aksum.

B. Write the letter of the name or term that best matches the description.

_____ **6.** An ancient African empire on the Horn of Africa

_____ **7.** Early peoples who slowly moved east and south across Africa

_____ **8.** One of the first Christian rulers

_____ **9.** A Kush ruler who conquered Egypt

_____ **10.** A region south of Egypt

a. Nubia

b. Nok

c. Aksum

d. Piankhi

e. Bantu

f. Ezana

READING STUDY GUIDE

Main Ideas

11. How did Nubia and Egypt exchange ways of life and ideas?

_____

_____

12. How did geography affect the development of Meroë as a trade city?

_____

_____

13. What two important changes did Ezana make for Aksum?

_____

_____

14. How did Aksum's farmers adapt to land?

_____

_____

15. What were the effects of the Bantu migration?

_____

_____

Thinking Critically

16. **Comparing** In what ways were Kush and Aksum alike?

_____

_____

17. **Making Inferences** How did the Kushites' war with the Assyrians show the importance of iron making?

_____

_____

Lesson 1 Geography and Indian Life

BEFORE YOU READ

In Lesson 1, you will learn how geography has influenced early Indian civilization.

AS YOU READ

Use this chart to record information about India's geography and early civilization.

Geography and Indian Life	
Physical geography of India	
Cities in the Indus Valley	
Harappan culture	

TERMS & NAMES

- **subcontinent** a large landmass that is like a continent, only smaller
- **Hindu Kush** a mountain range on the northern border of India
- **Himalayas** a mountain range on the northern border of India
- **monsoon** seasonal winds that help shape India's climate
- **Harappan civilization** an ancient Indus River culture
- **planned cities** cities that were built according to a design

Physical Geography of India

(pages 219–221)

How do mountains and seasonal winds shape the climate of India?

A **subcontinent** is a large landmass that is like a continent, but smaller. The subcontinent of South Asia includes present-day Bangladesh, Bhutan, India, Nepal, and most of India.

The **Hindu Kush** and the **Himalayas** are mountain ranges that form India's northern border. Several rivers are also part of the subcontinent. The Ganges and the Indus rivers are two of these rivers. Their water is used for irrigation. Silt from this water helps to make the land fertile. The first Indian civilization started in the Indus River valley. The Arabian Sea, the Indian Ocean, and the Bay of Bengal surround India. Ancient Indians used these waters to travel to other lands. This travel encouraged trade.

The mountains help to block cold winds from reaching India. So the climate there is warm. Seasonal winds called **monsoons** also influence India's climate. These winds cause a dry season in the winter and a rainy season in the summer. The rains sometimes cause great floods.

1. What factors affect the climate in India?

_____

_____

READING STUDY GUIDE CONTINUED

Cities in the Indus Valley

(pages 221–222)

Why was the earliest Indian civilization located near the Indus River?

Civilization in India began with farming along the Indus River. The early farmers raised wheat and barley. They also raised cotton. They were the first people in Asia to make cotton into fabric. Early people in India learned how to make copper and bronze tools.

People in the villages traded with one another. They also began to trade with people farther away. This trade helped to make them richer.

Some of these villages grew to be great cities. The best-known cities were Mohenjo-Daro and Harappa. The culture became known as the **Harappan civilization.**

The Harappan civilization was known for its **planned cities.** These cities were built according to a design. The streets in these cities crossed each other in grids. Brick walls surrounded the cities. The streets were lined with homes, shops, and factories. Almost every house in Harappan cities had a bathroom and a toilet. Underground sewers carried away the waste. Because Harappan cities were so well organized, historians believe the Harappans had strong leaders.

2. For what is the Harappan civilization known?

_____

_____

Harappan Culture

(pages 222–224)

What were the cultural features of Harappan civilization?

Harappans used about 500 pictographs, or picture signs, in their writing. Historians think that the pictographs may stand for words, sounds, or both. But no one has figured out how to read the writing.

Archaeologists have found evidence of religion in the Harappan culture. They think that a public bath in one of the cities may have been used for religious rituals. Archaeologists also found figures of animals. Today, Indians still view these figures as being holy.

Harappan culture spread across a large area. Historians found that cities in this area had a common design. People throughout the area used standard weights and measures. They had bronze statues and clay toys. Indians traded items such as timber for items such as silver and woolen cloth.

Historians think that around 2000 to 1500 B.C., the Indus Valley region experienced earthquakes. The earthquakes may have caused the Indus River to flood. People were forced to leave the cities. Soon the Harappan civilization declined.

3. What might have caused the Harappan civilization to decline?

_____

_____

READING STUDY GUIDE

Lesson 2 The Origins of Hinduism

BEFORE YOU READ

In Lesson 2, you will learn about the culture developed by the Aryan people in India.

AS YOU READ

Use an outline such as the one below to summarize each of the three main sections in the lesson.

> I. Aryans Move Into India
>
> II. Changes to Indian Life
>
> III. Hinduism: The Religion of India

TERMS & NAMES

- **Aryan** a group of Indo-Europeans
- **caste** a social class whose members are identified by their job
- **Brahmanism** the early religion of the Aryans
- **Hinduism** the major religion of India
- **reincarnation** the belief that each person has many lives
- **karma** a doctrine that believes what a person does in each life determines what he or she will be in the next life

---

Aryans Move Into India

(pages 227-228)

Who were the Aryans?

Indo-Europeans were nomads and herders from central Asia. They lived in family groups, or clans. They were warriors who rode chariots and fought with bows and arrows. Around 2000 b.c., the Indo-Europeans left their homes and moved to different regions. Historians do not know what caused them to move. Some settled in southwest Asia, others in parts of Europe.

Around 1500 b.c., a group of Indo-Europeans called **Aryans** moved into India. The Aryan way of life was different from the Harappans. The Harappans lived in cities.

The Aryans were herders who lived in simple houses. They spoke a language called Sanskrit.

1. In what parts of the world did Indo-Europeans settle?

   _____

   _____

   _____

READING STUDY GUIDE CONTINUED

Changes to Indian Life

(pages 228–229)

How was Aryan society organized?

The Aryans practiced a mysterious religion. As they moved slowly into India, they spread their religion and language. The Aryans interacted with other cultures in India. As a result, India developed a complex, blended culture.

Aryans were organized into three classes: warriors, priests, and commoners. These classes later developed into a caste system. A **caste** is a social class whose members are identified by their job. There were four major groups in the caste system. Eventually, a fifth group developed that was considered below all the other groups. This group came to be called the untouchables. They had to do the jobs no one else wanted.

The early religion of the Aryans is now known as **Brahmanism.** It included many nature gods. Brahmans made sacrifices to these gods. The rituals and hymns to these gods are found in texts called the Vedas. It is written in Sanskrit. Indians also wrote about their history in works such as the *Mahabharata.* This is a long poem that retells many legends.

2. What was the early religion of the Aryans?

   _____

   _____

   _____

Hinduism: The Religion of India

(pages 229–231)

How did the religion of Hinduism develop?

Hinduism is the major religion of India. It grew out of early Brahmanism. Hindus worship many gods, but they believe in one supreme God. They believe that other gods are parts of the one supreme God. The three most important of the other gods are Brahma, the creator; Vishnu, the protector; and Shiva, the destroyer.

Hindus believe in reincarnation. **Reincarnation** is the belief that each person has many lives. Hindus also follow a doctrine called **karma.** According to karma, what a person does in one life helps to decide what he or she will be in the next life. If a person is good, he or she may be reborn as a higher being. If a person is not good, he or she may be reborn as a lower being, such as a bug. Hindus believe in a cycle of birth, life, death, and rebirth. They believe the cycle ends only when a person reaches a union with God.

Hindus believe they can reach this union by following their own path. This involves doing one's job and carrying out the duties in life. To get closer to God, Hindus practice meditation to keep the mind calm. They also practice yoga, which includes exercise, breathing techniques, and diet.

3. How do Hindus believe they can reach a union with God?

   _____

   _____

   _____

   _____

READING STUDY GUIDE

Lesson 3 Buddhism and India's Golden Age

BEFORE YOU READ

In Lesson 3, you will learn about the start of Buddhism in India and about the advances made during the rule of the Guptas.

AS YOU READ

Use the diagram below to compare and contrast the Maurya and Gupta empires.

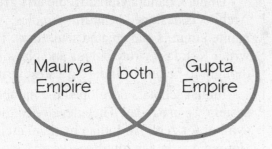

TERMS & NAMES
• **ahimsa** the practice of nonviolence
• **Buddhism** a religion based on the teachings of Siddhartha Gautama
• **Siddhartha Gautama** the Buddha, on whose teachings Buddhism is based
• **nirvana** the end of suffering
• **dharma** the collected teachings of Buddhism
• **Asoka** the greatest Maurya king

The Rise of Buddhism

(pages 233–235)

What are the main teachings of the religion of Buddhism?

In addition to Hinduism, other religions began in India. Jainism teaches **ahimsa,** which means "nonviolence." Jains believe that every living thing has a soul and should not be hurt. Another religion that began in India is **Buddhism.** It is based on the teachings of **Siddhartha Gautama.** When he began to teach, he was called the Buddha, or enlightened one.

Siddhartha was born a Hindu prince. After he saw troubles such as illness and poverty, he left his home to search for peace. After several years, he found understanding while meditating under a tree. He called this understanding the Four Noble Truths, which said:

People suffer because their minds are not at ease,

People are not at ease because they want what they don't have

People can stop suffering by not wanting what they don't have

People can stop wanting by following the Eightfold Path.

The path included such things as having the right opinions, actions, and meditation. Buddha taught that following this path could lead to **nirvana** or the end of suffering.

After Buddha died, his teachings were gathered together by his followers. These teachings are called the **dharma.** Monks and nuns are people who live in religious communities. They helped develop the formal religion of Buddhism. Over time, Buddhism split into many branches. Most Buddhists worshiped the Buddha as a divine being.

1. According to Buddha, how could people end their suffering?

_____

_____

_____

The Maurya Empire

(pages 235–236)

How did the Maurya rulers unite northern India into the first great Indian empire?

For hundreds of years, various Aryan kingdoms in India fought each other. Around 321 b.c., Chandragupta Maurya became king of one of the kingdoms. He began to conquer territory around his kingdom. Soon, the Maurya Empire covered much of India.

Chandragupta strictly controlled his empire. Many officials ran the government. To pay the officials, Chandragupta placed heavy taxes on the land and crops.

The greatest Maurya king was **Asoka,** Chandragupta's grandson. He started to rule in 269 b.c. Before long, Asoka conquered a neighboring kingdom. Then he began ruling according to Buddhist teachings. He gave up fighting and ruled peacefully by law.

Asoka sent out missionaries to spread Buddhism. But he also allowed people to practice other religions.

Buddhism became popular in India. For a while, fewer people worshiped Hindu gods. Hindu priests said their rituals in Sanskrit, which few people spoke anymore. So, many people turned to Buddhism.

But in the a.d. 600s, poets began to write hymns to the Hindu gods in the languages that most people spoke. These poems became popular across India. Soon people renewed their interest in Hinduism. At the same time, Buddhism began to decline. Soon it lost most of its followers in India. But by this time, Buddhism had spread to other countries in Asia.

2. How did Asoka rule the Maurya Empire?

_____

_____

_____

_____

The Golden Age of the Guptas

(pages 237–239)

Who were the Guptas, and when did they rule India?

After Asoka died, the Maurya Empire ended. Hundreds of years of fighting followed. Then the Gupta family took control. The greatest ruler of this family was Chandra Gupta II. During his rule (a.d. 375 to 415), India had a golden age. This age was a time of great accomplishments.

Under Chandra Gupta II, the arts grew. Architects designed beautiful temples. Artists painted murals and created sculptures. The writer Kalidasa wrote poems and plays. He is thought to be one of India's greatest writers.

Indian scholars developed the number system we use today. They developed the symbol for zero. An Indian mathematician figured out the length of one year.

Indian doctors added techniques to the practice of Ayurvedic medicine. It promotes good health by using diet, exercise, and other methods to keep up the body's energy.

Indian artisans were excellent metal workers. They made an iron pillar that stood almost 23 feet high. No other people were able to make such a large piece of iron until at least 1,000 years later.

Gupta India grew wealthy from trade. Traders sold goods to foreign merchants. Indian merchants bought Chinese goods, such as silk. They resold these goods to traders traveling west. Traders helped to spread Indian culture and beliefs to other parts of Asia.

3. What happened in India during Gupta rule?

_____

_____

_____

_____

READING STUDY GUIDE

CHAPTER 7 | LESSON 4 The Legacy of India

Lesson 4 The Legacy of India

BEFORE YOU READ

In Lesson 4, you will learn how Indian culture influences the modern world today.

AS YOU READ

Use a chart like this one to take notes about the legacy of India.

TERMS & NAMES
- **Mohandas Gandhi** Indian leader who used nonviolence in fighting British rule
- **Hindu-Arabic numerals** the numerals 1 to 9, which originated in India

Legacy of India

Religion	Arts	Mathematics

India's Religious Legacy

(pages 241–242)

How did the religions of India affect other cultures?

Most people in India today are Hindus. Hindus also live in many other countries, including the United States. Very few people in India practice Buddhism. But many people in other countries today practice Buddhism.

Hindu and Buddhist ideas have influenced many people. For example, the Indian leader **Mohandas Gandhi** used *ahimsa,* or nonviolence, to fight against British rule.

This happened in the mid-1900s. Hindu and Buddhist influences continue today. Many people from other religions meditate and practice yoga.

1. What are two ways in which Hindu and Buddhist influences can be seen today?

_____

_____

READING STUDY GUIDE

READING STUDY GUIDE CONTINUED

India's Artistic Legacy

(page 242)

How have the Indian arts influenced other cultures?

Indian arts have influenced other parts of the world. In many Southeast Asian nations, people perform plays based on the Sanskrit poem *Mahabharata.* Indian art and architecture have influenced other cultures. Indian artists have used symbols to show Buddha's holiness. Some of these symbols are still used today. An ancient Hindu temple in Cambodia shows Indian influences in the temple's design.

2. How has Indian architecture influenced other cultures?

_____

_____

_____

The Legacy of Indian Mathematics

(pages 242–243)

How does the mathematical knowledge of ancient India affect our lives today?

The numerals 1 to 9 that we use today were developed in India more than 2,000 years ago. Arab traders brought these numerals to the West. So they are called Arabic numerals, or **Hindu-Arabic numerals.**

The number system the Indians developed is called the decimal system. It is still used today. In this system, each numeral is worth ten times as much as the numeral to its right. The place of the numeral tells how much it is worth. The zero is an important symbol in the decimal system. The zero began to be used in India about 1,400 years ago.

3. What number system was developed in India that is used today?

_____

_____

_____

CHAPTER 7 | Ancient India

Chapter 7 Ancient India

Glossary/After You Read

chariot a cart with two wheels that is pulled by horses
doctrine a principle or belief that a religion holds to be true
enlightened having spiritual knowledge or understanding
flourish to do well, prosper
mysterious difficult to understand
place the position of a numeral
practice to follow the teachings of a religion
range a group of things in a line or row, such as mountains

Terms & Names

A. Circle the name or term that best completes each sentence.

1. India is a _____, which is like a continent, but smaller.

   monsoon   subcontinent   caste

2. India's climate is affected by seasonal winds called _____.

   monsoons   subcontinents   castes

3. Early Indian society was organized into social classes called _____.

   castes   karma   nirvana

4. _____ is a religion based on the teachings of Siddhartha Gautama.

   Buddhism   Hinduism   Sanskrit

5. A golden age in India occurred during the rule of the _____.

   Buddhists   Mauryas   Guptas

B. Write the letter of the name or term that best matches the description.

____ 6. mountain range that borders India on the north

____ 7. the river valley that was the site of the Harappan civilization

____ 8. the feature for which the Harappan civilization is known

____ 9. the greatest Maurya king

____ 10. the collected teachings of Buddha

a. Mohandas Gandhi
b. Himalayas
c. Asoka
d. dharma
e. Indus
f. planned cities

READING STUDY GUIDE

READING STUDY GUIDE CONTINUED

Main Ideas

11. How do India's rivers affect farming in the region?

_____

_____

12. How were the cities in the Harappan civilization unique?

_____

_____

13. How was Indian society organized?

_____

_____

14. What were two achievements of the Gupta Empire?

_____

_____

15. What two religions that started in India affect other cultures today?

_____

_____

Thinking Critically

16. **Drawing Conclusions** What do the planned cities of the Harappans tell about their civilization?

_____

_____

17. **Evaluating Information** What part of ancient Indian culture do you think has had the greatest effect on other cultures today? Why?

_____

_____

READING STUDY GUIDE

Lesson 1 Geography Shapes Life in Ancient China

BEFORE YOU READ

In this lesson, you will read about how geographic features shaped life in ancient China.

AS YOU READ

Use this graphic organizer to take notes on these geographic topics.

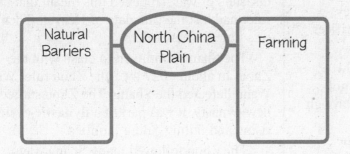

TERMS & NAMES

- **oracle bone** A piece of animal bone used to ask questions of and receive answers from the gods
- **pictograph** A simple drawing that stands for a word or idea
- **Mandate of Heaven** The belief in ancient China that a good ruler had the approval of the gods
- **dynastic cycle** The pattern of the rise and fall of dynasties in ancient China

The Geographic Features of China

(pages 253–254)

How was life in ancient China affected by the features of the land?

China is in eastern Asia. It is at about the same distance above the equator as the United States. The Yellow Sea, the East China Sea, and Pacific Ocean border China on the east. In the north is the Gobi Desert. The Taklimakan is in the west. Mountain ranges, like the Himalayas, form a curving border in the west.

Before modern transportation, this geography isolated China. China was not like the cultures on the Nile and in the Fertile Crescent. It did not exchange goods and ideas with other groups. Chinese civilization developed in its very own way.

In China, two major rivers flow to the Pacific Ocean. The Chang Jiang is in central China. It is also called the Yangtze. The Huang He is further north. It is also known as the Yellow River. Its floodwaters leave yellowish silt. This makes the soil very fertile. In ancient China, most farming was done in the very rich land between these two rivers. This area

is called the North China Plain. It has always been the center of Chinese civilization.

China has varied climates like the United States. The different climates make it possible to grow different kinds of crops. Rice is grown in the wet south. Wheat and *millet* are grown in the drier north.

1. Why did Chinese civilization develop on the North China Plain?

_____

_____

The Shang Dynasty

(pages 254–255)

How did the Chinese language develop?

Around 2000 B.C., cities began to develop along the Huang He. Chinese civilization grew there. Today, China's culture is based on that ancient civilization. This makes China the oldest continuing civilization in the world.

Around 1766 B.C., a family called the Shang began to rule. They set up a dynasty. The Shang kings carried out religious

activities. They claimed to rule with the gods' permission. The Shang did not have a central government. The kings controlled the central part of the North China Plain. Relatives ruled other areas. The Shang had chariots. They used them to defend themselves against nomads, like the Zhou.

Respect for parents was important in Shang culture. Fathers ruled the family. Family and religion were closely tied. Families paid respect to the spirits of the father's ancestors. They honored these ancestors with animal sacrifices. People believed this brought good luck.

The Shang kings claimed they could get the gods to help people. The kings got messages from the gods. These came through **oracle bones.** Royal priests scratched questions and answers on the bones. The scratch marks were an early form of writing.

The marks became a system of simple drawings called **pictographs.** Later, the pictographs turned into Chinese characters. Chinese writing uses a huge number of characters. An educated person needs to know at least 10,000. However, that person does not need to speak Chinese to be able to read the writing. Because of this, people speaking different types of Chinese can still use the same writing. This helped unite the large and varied country.

2. What system of writing did the Shang develop?

_____

_____

_____

_____

The Zhou Dynasty

(pages 255–257)

How did the Zhou conquer Shang lands?

Like other groups, Chinese people believed that rulers ruled by having the gods' favor. Good things happened when rulers were good. Bad things happened when rulers were bad. This idea became part of Chinese culture. It was called the **Mandate of Heaven.** When disasters or war happened this meant that the ruler had lost the Mandate of Heaven. Then it was time for new rulers.

The Shang continued to clash with the Zhou. In about 1027 B.C., the Zhou ruler Wu Wang defeated the Shang. The Zhou started a new dynasty. It was part of a **dynastic cycle** of rising and falling ruling families.

The Zhou followed many Shang ways. They did not have a central government. Zhou kings put family or trusted people in charge of some areas. These lords owed their loyalty to the king. They owed him their help during war, too. In return, the king promised to protect their lands.

When the lords grew stronger, they became less dependent on the king. They fought among themselves or with other groups. When they won, they expanded Chinese lands.

After 800 B.C., more nomads invaded China. In 771 B.C., they invaded the capital city of Hao. They killed the king. The king's family escaped. They set up a new capital at Luoyang. However, the king was now weak. The lords fought all the time. This led to a very bad period starting around 403 B.C. It is known as the Time of the Warring States.

3. How did the Mandate of Heaven help the Zhou take over China?

_____

_____

_____

Lesson 2 China's Ancient Philosophies

BEFORE YOU READ

In this lesson, you will read about three systems of thinking that developed in ancient China.

AS YOU READ

Use this diagram to compare the three systems of thinking you learn about in this lesson.

Legalism	Confucianism	Daoism

TERMS & NAMES

- **philosophy** A system of thinking
- **Legalism** A Chinese system of thinking that taught that the government must use the legal system to control people's behavior
- **Confucianism** A Chinese philosophy that teaches that society will run well if people behave properly
- **filial piety** Treating parents with respect
- **Daoism** A Chinese philosophy that teaches that a universal force, called the Dao, guides all things.

Legalism

(pages 259–260)

What was the main idea of Legalism?

The Time of the Warring States made people in China long for peace. Scholars wondered how to stop the fighting. They developed three ways of thinking, or **philosophies.** These were Legalism, Confucianism, and Daoism. People hoped that these philosophies would fix the problems in the land.

Legalism was the belief that rulers should use the legal system to force people to behave. People who followed this system thought society was in disorder. They believed that people are naturally wicked and can only be forced to be good. Legalists wanted the government to pass strict laws. They wanted harsh punishments to make people afraid to do wrong.

One legalist was Shang Yang. He wanted to make people report lawbreakers. If they did not, Shang Yang thought they should be cut in two. Other Legalists thought that a thief should be punished by having his foot cut off. Legalists also believed that the government

should reward people who did their duty.

Legalists did not want people to complain about government or question it. They thought people who did that should be arrested. They also taught that the government should burn books that held different ideas.

1. What did Legalists believe government must do?

_____

_____

Confucianism

(pages 260–261)

What did Confucius think would bring order to China?

Confucius was an important Chinese thinker. He lived from 551 to 479 B.C. This was a time of conflict and unrest. Confucius developed ideas to end conflict. His ideas are called **Confucianism.**

Confucius wanted to create peace in all *relationships*. His main idea was respect for

READING STUDY GUIDE CONTINUED

others. He believed if people treated each other well, there would be peace and harmony. Confucius also taught that leaders should set a good example for the people. His students collected his ideas into a book called the *Analects*.

In Confucianism there are five relationships. Each one has its own duties and code of proper conduct, or behavior. The five relationships fall into two main groups: proper conduct in the family and proper conduct in society.

Confucius believed that proper conduct began at home. Family members had to be good to one another. One of Confucius' most important teachings was about **filial piety.** This meant to treat one's parents with respect.

Proper conduct in society was also very important. People needed to be honest with friends. They should respect authority. Rulers must live correctly. They should treat their subjects fairly. A subject had a duty to obey a good, moral ruler. If people lived in these ways, then there would be peace in society.

Confucianism set out clear roles for the family and society. The Chinese people used this philosophy to avoid conflict and live in peace. Many rulers tried to live up to Confucius' ideas. Confucianism also encouraged learning. In this way, it laid the groundwork for fair and skilled government officials.

2. What did Confucius think would lead to peace in society?

_____

_____

_____

Daoism

(pages 262–263)

What was the main idea of Daoism?

A third major Chinese philosophy is **Daoism.** It may have been created by Laozi. No one knows if he existed. If he did, he lived in the 500s B.C. The book of his teachings is called the Dao De Jing. (The Book of the Way of Virtue.) Daoism is very different from Legalism and Confucianism.

Daoists believe in a universal force that guides all things. It is called the Dao, or the Way. All creatures, except people, live in harmony with the Dao. According to Daoism, people need to find their own way, or Dao, to live in peace. They must learn to live in harmony with nature. They must learn to live with their inner feelings, too.

Daoists did not worry about what is good or bad. They did not try to change things. They accepted life the way it is. They did not want to fix the government, either.

Daoists tried to live in harmony with nature and the universe. This included understanding the yin and the yang.

The yin and yang are the two sides of all things. The yin (black) stands for all that is cold, or dark, or mysterious. The yang (white) stands for all that is warm, bright, and light. Neither is bad or good. The yin and yang work together. They *complement* each other. Daoists taught that understanding yin and yang would help people understand their place in the world.

3. What did Daoists believe people should do?

_____

_____

_____

READING STUDY GUIDE

Lesson 3 The Qin and the Han

BEFORE YOU READ

In this lesson, you will read about two important early dynasties, the Qin and the Han.

AS YOU READ

Use this Venn diagram to take notes about the Qin and Han dynasties.

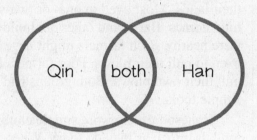

Qin both Han

TERMS & NAMES

- **Qin** A state in ancient China; later the name of a short-lived dynasty
- **Shi Huangdi** The first Qin emperor
- **Han Dynasty** An important Chinese dynasty that ruled from 202 B.C. to 220 A.D.
- **bureaucracy** A government system of chosen officials

The Qin Unified China

(pages 267–268)

How did the Qin unify China?

At the end of the time of Zhou rule, some lords were still at war. This showed people that the Zhou no longer had the Mandate of Heaven. A new ruler was needed.

The new ruler was from an area called **Qin.** The name China may have come from this word. This new Qin ruler took the name **Shi Huangdi.**

In 221 B.C., Shi Huangdi began to stop the battles between the warring lords. He then conquered rival states. He drove out the nomadic invaders, too. China grew.

Shi Huangdi was a Legalist. He tried to wipe out Confucian thinking. He had Confucian followers killed. He burned books that contained ideas he did not like.

As a Legalist, Shi Huangdi wanted a strong central government. He also wanted to control it himself. To do this, he went after the lords. He took away some of their lands. He forced them to live in his capital so he could watch them. In this way, he weakened the noble families and increased his power.

Shi Huangdi also united the lands he controlled. He built highways and irrigation systems. He forced the peasants to work on these projects. He set high taxes to pay for them. He also set standards for weights, measures, coins, and writing. These steps drew the lands together. It made it easier to trade and do business throughout China.

Another of Shi Huangdi's projects was a long wall. It was to keep invaders from crossing China's northern borders.

This first Great Wall linked smaller walls. They had been built during the Time of the Warring States. The earlier walls were built of earth. The new wall was made of stone and brick. Thousands of peasants and criminals were forced to work on this wall. Many died from it. People became angry about this.

Shi Huangdi died in 210 B.C. He was buried in a complex tomb. An army of baked-clay soldiers was buried with him. Archaeologists discovered this tomb in 1974.

1. Why did Shi Huangdi build highways and set government standards?

_____

_____

_____

The Han Dynasty

(pages 269–270)

How did the Han rule China?

Shi Huangdi's son was weak. People *rebelled* under his rule. A civil war broke out, too. Eventually, a military leader took control. His name was Liu Bang. He ended the civil war and reunited China. He also started the **Han Dynasty** in 202 B.C. This dynasty ruled until about 220 A.D. The Han emperors ruled China during the same time that the Roman Empire ruled in the west.

Liu Bang kept the central government strong. However, he lowered taxes. He made punishments less harsh, too. In Han times, peasant men owed the government a month of labor per year. This was to work on the ruler's public projects. The peasants worked to build roads and canals. They built irrigation systems, too.

The Han set up a **bureaucracy.** The officials in the bureaucracy helped enforce Han rule. The Han put family members and trusted people in local governments. They set up a system of tests. These tests helped find the best-educated and most moral people to work in the government. The tests checked people's knowledge of Confucian beliefs.

Liu Bang died in 195 B.C. Then his widow, the Empress Lü, took over. She ruled for their young son. Lü outlived her son. She kept putting infants on the throne so that she could stay in power. When she died in 180 B.C., everyone in her family was executed. From 141 to 87 B.C. a descendant of Liu Bang ruled China. His name was Wudi. He was called the *"Martial Emperor."* This was because he used war to expand China. Wudi conquered southern China, northern Vietnam, and northern Korea. He forced the nomads out of the north. Wudi greatly enlarged China.

2. What new system did the Han rulers set up?

    _____

    _____

Life in Han China

(pages 270–271)

What was life like in China under Han rule?

Many Chinese today call themselves "people of the Han." They *identify* with the times under Han rule. The Han were hard working. They created a successful civilization.

A large number of the people during Han times were farmers. They lived in villages near their lands. Most lived in one- or two-story mud homes. Barns and other out buildings were nearby. Rich farmers might have had oxen to pull their plows. Poor farmers had to pull their own plows. Both groups had a few simple tools.

Chinese farmers wore simple clothing and sandals, much as they do today. When it got cold, they stuffed their clothing like a quilt. Northern farmers grew millet and wheat. In the south they grew rice. Families kept vegetable gardens for extra food. People could get fish and meat, but it cost a lot. Most people only ate small amounts of fish and meat.

Not everyone lived in the country, however. Han China had great cities, too. They were centers of trade, learning, and government. Merchants, craftspeople, and government workers lived in the cities. In some ways, these cities were like today's cities. They were crowded. There were fun things to do. Entertainment included music, juggling, and acrobatics. Unfortunately, they may also have had street gangs.

3. During Han times, how was life in the country different from life in the city?

    _____

    _____

    _____

    _____

    _____

CHAPTER 8 | LESSON 4 The Legacy of Ancient China

Lesson 4 The Legacy of Ancient China

BEFORE YOU READ

In this lesson, you will read about the lasting contributions of ancient China.

AS YOU READ

Use this diagram to take record details about China's legacy.

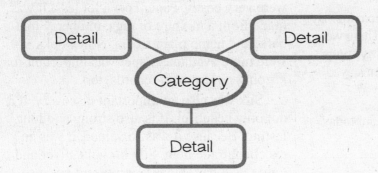

TERMS & NAMES
- **Silk Roads** Overland trade routes from Asia to Europe
- **trans-Eurasian** Across Europe and Asia
- **cultural diffusion** The spread of ideas and customs

The Silk Roads

(pages 277–278)

What kinds of goods moved along the Silk Roads?

During Han rule, only the Chinese knew how to make silk. People outside China very much wanted this *luxury* cloth. In this way, silk was important in opening trade routes to the west.

Major trade routes became known as **Silk Roads.** Merchants carried silk and other goods on these highways. These **trans-Eurasian** routes stretched from Asia to Europe. China was no longer isolated. It was part of a huge global trade network.

By 100 B.C., the Silk Roads were well known and well traveled. Goods coming out of China included silk, paper, and pottery. Goods coming to China from the west included *sesame* seeds and oil, metals, and gems. The Chinese also prized Central Asian horses.

Ideas and customs also moved along the Silk Roads. This **cultural diffusion** brought things like military methods and cultural styles

to China. In turn, Chinese art, silk, and pottery influenced peoples in the west.

During the Han period Buddhism also spread along the Silk Roads. Missionaries from India brought Buddhism to China. From there it spread to Japan and Korea. Chinese Buddhists changed the religion to make it fit better with their own ways of living.

1. How did the Silk Roads help spread Buddhism?

_____

_____

_____

READING STUDY GUIDE

READING STUDY GUIDE CONTINUED

Influential Ideas and Beliefs

(page 278)

How important were Confucianism and Daoism?

Confucian standards remained important in Chinese government and learning. Today, Confucius' ideas are still followed in Chinese villages. Confucianism also became very important in Japan, Korea, and Vietnam.

Daoism had a lasting effect on China, too. By the 500s A.D., it was a major religion. There were Daoist priests, rituals, and many, many writings. Unlike Confucianism, however, Daoism stayed mainly in China.

2. How is Confucianism still important today?

_____

_____

_____

Chinese Inventions and Discoveries

(pages 279–280)

What advances did the Han make?

Ancient China had a huge and growing population. It had to find ways to feed everyone. Because of this, many important Chinese inventions at this time were related to farming.

For example, the Chinese came up with a better plow. They made improved farm tools, too. These helped increase crops. The invention of a collar harness helped horses to pull heavier loads. The wheelbarrow made it easier for farmers to move loads by hand. Watermills used river power to grind grain.

The Chinese invented paper in A.D. 105. Before that, books were made of silk. They were very costly. Paper cost a lot less. It was made from a mixture of rags, mulberry tree bark, and hemp plant fibers. Now books were more available. Paper was important for keeping government records, too.

Silk was also an important discovery. It is not only beautiful. It is also strong and long lasting. Because it was so valued, it was an excellent trade item. Silk brought silver and gold to China. This was important because China did not have much of these metals itself. At one time, one pound of silk was worth one pound of gold.

3. What inventions did the Han make that improved farming?

_____

_____

_____

_____

Chapter 8 Ancient China

Glossary/After You Read

complement to work well with

conduct the way someone acts; behavior

favor support or approval

harness a set of straps used to attach an animal to a plow or vehicle

identify to see oneself as part of a group

luxury beyond what is needed to live; something that is finely made or expensive

martial having to do with fighting or war

millet a plant the people grow for its grain

nomad a person who moves from place to place

rebel to defy authority

relationship a tie between people or things

rival in competition with

sesame a plant with small seeds that can be made into oil or used for flavoring

standard a model rule or practice

wicked mean, bad, or evil

Terms & Names

A. Circle the name or term that best completes each sentence.

1. Shang priests used _____ to ask questions of the gods.

   bureaucracy   oracle bones   philosophy

2. When the Han took over China from the Qin they began a _____.

   cultural diffusion   philosophy   dynastic cycle

3. Chinese writing developed from a system of _____.

   filial piety   pictographs   bureaucracy

4. A(n) _____ is a system of thinking.

   philosophy   bureaucracy   oracle bone

5. The spreading of customs and ideas is called _____.

   philosophy   filial piety   cultural diffusion

B. Write the letter of the name that best matches the description.

_____ 6. The system of thought that teaches that there is a universal force

_____ 7. The belief that a leader rules by the favor of the gods

_____ 8. The system of thought that teaches the importance of respect and proper conduct

_____ 9. A state in ancient China

_____ 10. The system of thought that teaches the need for strong laws and harsh punishments

a. Mandate of Heaven
b. Shi Huangdi
c. Legalism
d. Daoism
e. Confucianism
f. Qin

READING STUDY GUIDE

READING STUDY GUIDE CONTINUED

Main Ideas

11. Why was ancient China isolated at first?

_____

_____

12. What has always been the center of Chinese civilization?

_____

_____

13. What is the main idea in Confucianism?

_____

_____

14. What were the achievements of the Han emperor Wudi?

_____

_____

15. What are three Chinese inventions that still exist today?

_____

_____

Thinking Critically

16. Making Inferences Why do you think Shi Huangdi was a Legalist?

_____

_____

17. Understanding Cause and Effect How did the invention of silk change ancient China?

_____

_____

_____

Lesson 1 The Geography of the Americas

BEFORE YOU READ

In this lesson, you will learn about the kind of environment early people faced in the Andes and in Mesoamerica.

AS YOU READ

Use this diagram to compare the geography of the Andes with the geography of Mesoamerica.

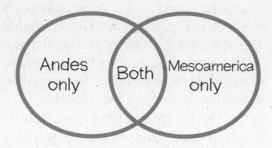

TERMS & NAMES

- **isthmus** narrow land bridge that connects two larger bodies of land
- **tropical** areas that are warm and rainy
- **Mesoamerica** region in North America that includes southern Mexico and parts of Central America
- **Yucatán Peninsula** area of land that lies between the Gulf of Mexico and the Pacific Ocean
- **slash-and-burn agriculture** technique of clearing land by cutting back and burning it

Physical Geography of the Americas

(pages 289–290)

What is the physical geography of the Americas like?

The continents of North and South America are connected by an **isthmus,** which is a narrow land bridge. However, the geography and climate of the two continents are very different.

Mountains are found on the western part of both continents. They run from north to south. The mountain range in North America is called the Rocky Mountains. The mountain range in South America is called the Andes. Water from the mountains flow into rivers. The Mississippi is the major river system in North America. The Amazon and Paraná are the major river systems in South America.

North America is located above the equator and South America is below it. Most of North America has a mild climate with

four seasons. Most people live in the areas with the mild climate. Some parts of North America are very cold.

South America also has many different climates. Much of South America receives a great amount of rain. About half of South America is warm and rainy. These areas are called tropical. Some parts of North America are also **tropical.** They are in Central America. Early people built ancient civilizations in these tropical areas.

1. In what part of North America and South America are different mountain ranges located?

_____

_____

_____

READING STUDY GUIDE

Geography of the Andes

(pages 290–291)

What geographic features are characteristic of the Andes?

Ancient civilization started in the Andes Mountains of South America. The peaks of these mountains are the highest in the Americas. The Andes are located where two plates bump together. The movement causes volcanic activity and earthquakes in the Andes. In the high parts of these mountains, temperatures can be very cold and rainfall is unpredictable.

In parts of the Andes, the mountains split into two ranges. High plateaus are found between them. The plateaus include deserts and landforms such as hills, valleys, and plains.

Because of the harsh environment, ancient farmers in the Andes developed irrigation canals. They grew crops, such as potatoes.

2. Why do earthquakes often occur in the Andes?

_____

_____

_____

_____

Geography of Mesoamerica

(pages 292–293)

How do the geography and climate of Mesoamerica contrast with those of the Andes?

Mesamerica is a region in North America that includes southern Mexico and parts of Central America. Mesamerica has two main regions. They are the highlands and lowlands. The tropical lowlands are areas of jungle found along the coast of the Gulf of Mexico. They are also found on the **Yucatán Peninsula,** which is located between the Gulf of Mexico and the Pacific Ocean. The highlands of Mesoamerica are located between mountains called the Sierra Madre. The area often has volcanic activity and earthquakes.

The lowlands receive more than 100 inches of rain each year. The highlands have a cooler and drier climate. In the drier highlands, early farmers had to irrigate their fields. They grew corn, beans, and squash. In the lowlands, farmers used **slash-and-burn agriculture.** They used this technique to clear parts of the jungle and burn it

3. What are the two main regions of Mesoamerica?

_____

_____

_____

_____

READING STUDY GUIDE

CHAPTER 9 | LESSON 2 Ancient Andean Civilizations

Lesson 2 Ancient Andean Civilizations

BEFORE YOU READ

In this lesson, you will learn about the early civilizations that developed in the harsh environment of the Andes.

AS YOU READ

Use a diagram like the one below to draw conclusions about the three ancient Andean civilizations as you read Lesson 2.

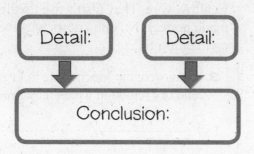

TERMS & NAMES
- **Chavín** ancient culture of the Andes region united mainly by religion
- **textile** woven cloth
- **Nazca** ancient culture that arose along the southern coast of present-day Peru
- **aquifer** an underground water source
- **Moche** ancient culture that arose along Peru's northern coast

The Chavín Civilization

(pages 295–296)

What was the Chavín civilization?

The **Chavín** culture flourished around 900 to 200 B.C. in the Andes of Peru. What people know about this culture comes from ruins found in a place called Chavín de Huantar. Most of the ruins have to do with religious structures and images.

Chavín de Huantar was most likely a religious center. Chavín priests probably had farmers, who made up most of Chavín society, build the city. The Chavín culture probably spread to northern and central Peru. Archaeologists have found the Chavín art style there in stone carvings, pottery, and in woven cloth called **textiles.**

1. What was Chavín de Huantar probably used for?

_____

_____

The Nazca Civilization

(pages 296–297)

How did the Nazca adapt to their harsh environment?

The **Nazca** culture arose along the southern coast of present-day Peru. It existed from around 200 B.C. to A.D. 600.

Not much is known about the Nazca culture. What people do know is that the Nazca were farmers in a region that received less than an inch of rain a year. So they built a large system of underground canals to water their crops.

The Nazca made beautiful pottery and textiles made of wool. The wool came from the alpaca, a camel-like animal. The Nazca are also known for the drawings they etched into the plains of southeastern Peru. The drawings are known as the Nazca Lines. No one knows what the lines were for. Some people believe that the drawings were made to please the gods. Other people believe the lines showed where **aquifers,** or underground water sources, were located.

READING STUDY GUIDE

READING STUDY GUIDE CONTINUED

2. What do people think was the purpose of the Nazca Lines?

_____

_____

_____

The Moche Civilization

(pages 298–299)

What does Moche art tell us about their civilization?

The **Moche** civilization arose on the northern coast of Peru. It existed from around A.D. 100 to 700. The city of Moche was probably the capital of the Moche civilization.

The region where the Moche people lived was hot and dry. So the farmers channeled the rivers from the Andes Mountains into irrigation systems to water their crops. They grew many different crops. They also fished and hunted game.

The Moche were skilled architects. They built temples, some of which still stand today. The temples may have been the centers of Moche government. Nobles ruled the people. The lower classes, made up of farmers and workers, paid taxes to repair the temples and other buildings.

Archaeologists have learned much about the Moche from objects found in their tombs. The Moche made jewelry, which the wealthy wore. They also wove textiles and made pottery. No one knows why the Moche civilization fell.

3. How were the Moche able to farm in the hot and dry region in which they lived?

_____

_____

_____

READING STUDY GUIDE

Lesson 3 The Olmec of Mesoamerica

BEFORE YOU READ

In this lesson, you will learn about the Olmec, the first civilization that developed in Mesoamerica.

AS YOU READ

Use a web diagram like the one below to describe the cities, culture, and legacy of the Olmec.

TERMS & NAMES
- **Olmec** first known civilization in Mesoamerica
- **mother culture** a culture that supported and influenced other cultures

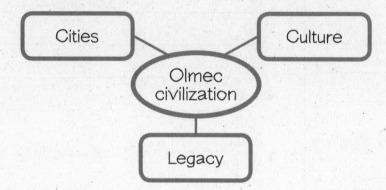

The Earliest American Civilization

(pages 301–302)

What helped the Olmec develop the first civilization in the Americas?

The **Olmec** is the first known civilization in Mesoamerica. The Olmec lived in the jungles along the Gulf coast of southern Mexico. Olmec farmers grew corn in the rich soil found along the rivers in the region.

The Olmec built several great cities. In one city, archaeologists have found earth mounds and pyramids. Archaeologists believe that powerful dynasties ruled Olmec cities. Engineers, builders, and artists made up the social class below the rulers. Farmers made up the largest and lowest social class in the Olmec civilization.

1. Where was the Olmec civilization located?

_____

_____

_____

_____

Olmec Culture

(pages 302–303)

What did the Olmec accomplish in art and learning?

The Olmec created some amazing art. Archaeologists have found huge stone heads, some as high as 9 feet and weighing as much as 20 tons. The heads were made using simple tools. Archaeologists think the heads may be of rulers or gods, but they do not know for sure.

Olmec art was often tied to religion. The Olmec worshiped many nature gods. One of their most important gods was the jaguar.

READING STUDY GUIDE

Many Olmec sculptures show creatures that are half human and half jaguar.

Archaeologists believe that the Olmec developed a calendar to keep track of religious ceremonies. They may also have used picture symbols.

2. Why do archaeologists believe that the jaguar was an important god in the Olmec culture?

_____

_____

_____

_____

Olmec Legacy

(pages 303–304)

How did the Olmec influence other cultures?
The Olmec civilization ended around 400 B.C. It may have been destroyed by invaders. But the Olmec influenced other Meso-American cultures. As a result, the Olmec are often called Mesoamerica's **mother culture.** The Olmec's large trading network helped to spread its culture.

Olmec art styles influenced the art of other cultures. The pottery and jewelry of other cultures feature the jaguar. The Olmec also influenced the kinds of cities and ceremonial centers that later cultures built. The Olmec's use of picture writing may have influenced later writing systems.

3. How has the Olmec culture influenced the art of later cultures?

_____

_____

_____

_____

Lesson 4 The Mayan Civilization

BEFORE YOU READ

In this lesson, you will learn about the Maya, who built a powerful civilization in Mesoamerica.

AS YOU READ

As you read each subsection, summarize it by identifying the main ideas and detail in a diagram like the one below.

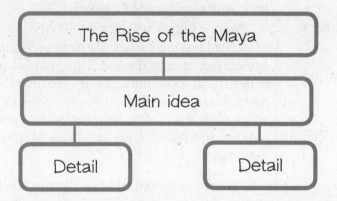

The Rise of the Maya

Main idea

Detail   Detail

TERMS & NAMES
- **Maya** a powerful civilization of Mesoamerica
- **maize** a type of corn
- **stele** a carved stone slab
- **glyph** a symbolic picture
- **codex** a bark-paper book in which important historical events were recorded

The Rise of the Maya

(pages 307–308)

Where did Mayan civilization rise?

The Mayan civilization began while the Olmec declined. It stretched from southern Mexico into northern Central America. The area included lowlands in the north and highlands in the south.

The **Maya** began to settle in the lowlands around 1500 B.C. They were farmers and traders. The Maya practiced their religion in ceremonial centers located in villages. The villages then developed into cities.

The Maya made their greatest accomplishments from about A.D. 250 to 900. This time is called the Classic Period. During this time, the Maya built great city-states that had temples, pyramids, and plazas. Each city-state was ruled by its own king. But the cities were connected to one another through trade.

1. Why is the time between A.D. 250 and 900 known as the Mayan Classic Period?

_____

_____

_____

Mayan Life

(pages 308–309)

How was Mayan society structured?

The Maya had a clear social structure. At the top was the king. He was followed by the noble class. Merchants and artisans came next. They were followed by farmers and then slaves.

Most Mayan people were farmers. They grew beans and a type of corn called **maize.** Corn was important to the Maya because they believed that people had been created out of maize.

The Maya dug canals to carry water from lowland swamp water to their fields. They added

added the soil from the canal beds to keep their fields above river level. They built their houses on poles to keep the houses above the ground and dry. In contrast, members of the noble class lived in stone palaces. They wore beautiful clothes and jewelry.

Religion was important in Mayan life. The Maya had many gods. Their most important god was the god of fire. To please the gods, the Maya made offerings of animals and plants. Sometimes they even made human offerings. The Maya also played a ritual ball game on a big court. They believed that playing the game would bring the rain they needed.

2. Why was maize an important crop to the Maya?

_____

_____

_____

_____

Mayan Culture

(pages 309–311)

What were Mayan achievements in art and learning?

Mayan art was linked to religion. The Maya left behind pottery, sculpture, and **steles.** These are carved stone slabs. They were used to mark special religious dates. They were also used to honor the reign of a ruler.

The Maya, like the ancient Indians, used a symbol for the zero. They also used positions to show place. The Maya used their knowledge of mathematics to develop a calendar. Their 365-day calendar was almost as accurate as the calendar people use today.

The Maya created the most advanced writing system in ancient America. They used **glyphs,** or symbolic pictures, to stand for whole words, syllables, and sounds. They used the glyphs to record important events in a bark-paper book called a **codex.**

No one knows why, but by 900 the Maya had left their cities. Perhaps wars had caused the cities to decline. They may have experienced food shortages. By the time the Spanish arrived in the 1500s, only weak city-states were left. Today, however, Mayan people still live in Mesoamerica and speak Mayan languages.

3. What mathematical ideas did the Maya develop?

_____

_____

_____

_____

Chapter 9 Ancient America

Glossary/After You Read

beds the grounds under bodies of water

engineers people who make practical use of scientific knowledge to design and build things

impact an effect

landforms natural features of the land, such as mountains

legacy something passed down from an ancestor or predecessor

plazas public squares in a town or city

ruins the remains of something that has been destroyed or has decayed

severe very harsh or extreme

tomb a grave, chamber, or structure for holding a dead body

wool the soft, thick, often curly hair of sheep and other animals

Terms & Names

A. Write the letter of the names or term that best matches the descriptions.

_____ **1.** underground water sources

_____ **2.** woven cloth

_____ **3.** a narrow land bridge

_____ **4.** a type of corn

_____ **5.** warm and rainy areas

a. isthmus

b. tropical

c. aquifers

d. textiles

e. mother culture

f. maize

B. Circle the name or term that best completes each sentence.

6. _____ are the landforms that run along the western part of both North America and South America.

       plateaus   mountains   plains

7. About half of South America has a _____ climate.

       tropical   severe   mild

8. The _____ culture developed along Peru's northern coast.

       Nazca   Mayan   Moche

9. The _____ culture is considered to be Mesoamerica's mother-culture.

       Chavin   Olmec   Mayan

10. Mayan writing used symbolic pictures called _____.

       steles   maize   glyphs

READING STUDY GUIDE

Main Ideas

11. What are the two major river systems of North and South America?

_____

_____

12. Why did Mesoamerican farmers practice slash-and-burn agriculture?

_____

_____

13. How have archaeologists learned about Moche civilization?

_____

_____

14. How was Olmec society organized?

_____

_____

15. What were the possible causes for the decline of the Mayan civilization?

_____

_____

Thinking Critically

16. **Comparing and Contrasting** Compare the geography and climate of North America and South America.

_____

_____

_____

17. **Making Decisions** Which Meso-American civilization would you choose to visit? Why?

_____

_____

_____

CHAPTER 10 | LESSON 1 The Origins of the Hebrews

Lesson 1 The Origins of the Hebrews

BEFORE YOU READ

In this lesson, you will read about the origins of the Hebrew people and their early history.

AS YOU READ

Use this graphic organizer to record the effects of some events in early Hebrew history.

Causes	Effects
Abraham leaves Ur.	
Moses leads people out of Egypt.	
Moses climbs Mount Sinai.	

TERMS & NAMES
- **Abraham** The father of the Hebrews
- **monotheism** A belief in one all-powerful God
- **Judaism** The name of the Hebrews' religion today
- **Moses** A Hebrew leader who led them out of Egypt
- **Exodus** The migration of the Hebrews out of Egypt
- **Ten Commandments** Ten laws given by God to Moses and the Hebrews

The Hebrew People in Canaan

(pages 325–326)

What is the central belief of the Hebrews?

The Hebrews were an early people in Southwest Asia. Later they were known as the Israelites. Today they are the Jews. The first five books of their Bible are called the Torah. It holds the early history, laws, and beliefs of the Hebrews.

Abraham is the father of the Hebrews. The Torah says that long ago God spoke to Abraham. He was a *shepherd* in Ur, in Mesopotamia. God told Abraham to leave Ur and go to Canaan. God *promised* Canaan to Abraham and his descendants. Abraham took his family and settled in this "Promised Land."

In ancient times, most people believed in many gods. The Hebrews were the first to believe in one all-powerful God. This is **monotheism.** Today, the Hebrews' religion is called **Judaism.**

During bad times, the Hebrews kept their belief in their covenant with God. A covenant is a binding agreement. They took courage from God's pledge to give the people of

Abraham a homeland if they followed the laws of their faith.

1. What was new about the religion of the Hebrews?

_____

_____

_____

Canaan to Egypt and Back

(pages 326–328)

Why did the Hebrews go to Egypt?

After living in Canaan for a time, the Hebrews renamed themselves the Israelites. This name came from Abraham's grandson, Jacob. After Jacob fought with one of God's messengers, he was given the name "Israel." Jacob had 12 sons.

The Torah says there was a terrible famine in Canaan. The starving Israelites went to Egypt. There, Jacob's son Joseph became a top adviser to the pharaoh.

Later another pharaoh came to power. He enslaved the Israelites. He forced them to work

on his building projects. The Torah tells how a leader named **Moses** helped the Israelites leave Egypt. Their journey out of Egypt is called the **Exodus.**

Once away, the Israelites spent 40 years wandering in the Sinai Desert. The Torah tells that at this time Moses climbed Mount Sinai. There, God spoke to him and gave him two stone tablets. The tablets contained the **Ten Commandments.** These ten rules became the basis of the Israelites' social and religious laws.

The Ten Commandments strengthened the covenant between God and the Israelites. God would protect the Israelites and they, in turn, would obey his rules. The Israelites believed that God used the Ten Commandments to set down moral laws for all people.

2. What happened to the Israelites in Egypt?

_____

_____

_____

Return to the Promised Land

(pages 328–329)

What role did the judges play in the life of ancient Israel?

The Israelites were gone from Canaan for many years. In the meantime, other peoples also lived in Canaan. These included the Canaanites and the Hittites. The Israelites would have to fight to regain Canaan.

Before Moses died, he picked a man named Joshua to lead the people back into Canaan. All the Israelites were descendants of Jacob. They were grouped into 12 tribes. Each tribe was named after one of Jacob's sons or grandsons. The men of the tribes became Joshua's troops. They were united in their goal of regaining the land. The fighting lasted for 200 years.

After Joshua died, and the wars went on, the Israelites did not pick another single strong leader. Instead, they got leadership from highly respected people of the community. These were the judges.

The first judges were military leaders. Later judges gave advice on the law. They also helped to settle conflicts. Judges such as Gideon, Samson, and Samuel gained *fame* for their strength and wisdom. Deborah was a very famous judge. She inspired a small group of fighters to win a battle against a large group of Canaanites.

The judges played a key role in keeping the 12 tribes united. When the Israelites did not have a strong judge, some tribes turned away from traditional religion. They worshiped figures of other gods. The judges spoke out against this.

Once the Israelites had Canaan back, they became farmers and herders. Each tribe received a part of the land. Some lived in the mountains. Others lived on the plains. Tribes that lived near each other formed close ties.

3. Why did the Israelites have to fight when they returned to Canaan?

_____

_____

_____

CHAPTER 10 | LESSON 2 Kingdoms and Captivity

Lesson 2 Kingdoms and Captivity

BEFORE YOU READ

In this lesson, you will read about the early kingdoms of Israel and Judah.

AS YOU READ

Use this graphic organizer to record the important events in the early Israelite kingdoms.

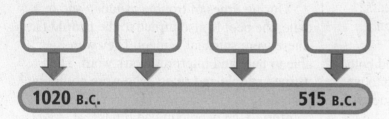

TERMS & NAMES
• **David** A king of Israel chosen by Samuel
• **Solomon** A major king of Israel and son of David
• **Babylonian Captivity** The 50-year period when the Jews were exiled in Babylon
• **Messiah** A chosen leader and heir to David's throne sent by God
• **prophet** A spiritual leader who can interpret God's word

The Kingdom of Israel

(pages 335–336)

Who were some of the early kings of Israel?

The Israelites were different from other peoples in the region. Their worship of one God and other beliefs set them apart. They traded with other groups in Canaan. However, they did not take on their ways.

About 1029 B.C., the Israelites faced the Philistines, another people in the area. The Israelites agreed to unite under one king in order to fight the Philistines.

In 1020 B.C., the Israelites chose Saul as their first king. He was a strong military leader. Under Saul, the Israelites fought the Philistines. They won back some control of their land.

Before he died, Saul chose the next king. His name was **David.** In about 1000 B.C., David led the Israelites in driving out the Philistines. David won control of Jerusalem, too.

David started a dynasty. He chose his son **Solomon** to be king after him. In about 962 B.C., Solomon became the third king of Israel. He was a very strong leader.

During Solomon's rule, Israel became powerful. Solomon built on existing trade ties. He also made new ones. He oversaw many building projects, too. The most famous is the Temple in Jerusalem. The Temple became the center of religious life for the Israelites. People came from everywhere in the kingdom to worship there. They also came to ask the wise king to settle disputes.

1. Who were David and Solomon?

_____

_____

_____

_____

The Kingdom Divides

(page 337)

What was the outcome of the conflict among the Israelites?

Faced with the threat of the Philistines, the tribes of Israel had united. When the threat

READING STUDY GUIDE

was gone, they fought each other. In 922 B.C., Solomon died. The northern tribes would not pledge loyalty to his son. They wanted him to lower their taxes and end forced labor. When he refused, the northern tribes rebelled. Only the tribes of Judah and Benjamin stayed loyal.

Israel now split into two kingdoms. The northern part was still called Israel. The southern part was now called Judah. Jerusalem was in Judah. The words Judaism and Jews come from the name Judah. The two kingdoms were separate for about two hundred years. During this time, Jerusalem remained an important center of worship.

In 738 B.C., the Assyrians threatened both countries. They forced Israel and Judah to pay tribute. In 722 B.C., the Assyrians conquered Israel.

In 612 B.C., the New Babylonians conquered the Assyrian lands. In 586 B.C., the king of Babylon, Nebuchadnezzar, captured Jerusalem. Judah's leaders resisted his rule, so the Babylonians destroyed the Temple. They took thousands of Jews to Babylon as slaves.

2. Why did Israel split into two kingdoms?

_____

_____

_____

Jewish Exiles Return to Judah

(pages 338–339)

What hope sustained the Jews in exile?

The Israelites were kept in Babylon for about 50 years. This period is called the **Babylonian Captivity.** During the Captivity, the Israelites became known as the Jews.

While in Babylon, the Jews worked hard to keep their identity. They kept their practices, holy days, and beliefs. They hoped one day to return to Judah. They wanted to rebuild the Temple, too.

In exile, the Jews hoped to have their own king again. Before the Captivity, priests would bless, or anoint, a new ruler. So one title for the king was **Messiah.** It means an "anointed one." The exiles believed that God would send the Messiah to unite the people.

During times of trouble in Judah and in exile, the people also turned to the **prophets.** These were spiritual leaders. They were able to hear and interpret God's word. They warned people and rulers who were not living according to God's laws. The prophets also comforted the people in bad times.

In 539 B.C., the Persians conquered the Babylonians. The Persian king Cyrus freed the Jews. They returned to Judah. Very quickly, they began rebuilding the Temple in Jerusalem. This Second Temple was finished in 515 B.C. The people now looked forward to a time when they would be independent.

3. Who were the prophets?

_____

_____

_____

_____

CHAPTER 10 | LESSON 3 Rome and Judea

Lesson 3 Rome and Judea

BEFORE YOU READ

In this lesson, you will read about conquests of Judea by Syria and Rome.

AS YOU READ

Use this Venn diagram to take notes about how the Syrians and Romans each treated Jewish struggles against their rule.

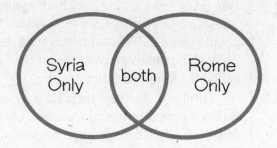

TERMS & NAMES
- **Diaspora** The movement of Jews out of Judea to other parts of the world
- **rabbi** A religious leader and teacher
- **synagogue** A Jewish place of worship and prayer

Ruled by Foreigners

(pages 343–344)

What was the relationship of Judah to Syria?

Judah's location put it in the path of conquering armies. In 198 B.C., the Syrians took over Judah. Syrian rulers liked Greek culture. They brought Greek ideas and beliefs into Judah. Some Jews took on Greek ways of life. Some began to worship Greek gods. Most did not, however. They still followed Jewish beliefs and ways.

At first Syrian rulers let the Jews keep their own ways. In 175 B.C., however a new ruler came to power. He ordered Jewish priests to make offerings to Greek gods. When they refused, this ruler outlawed the Jews' religion. He put Greek statues in the Temple in Jerusalem. He made it a crime to observe Jewish laws or study the Torah. Some Jews fled to the hills. There, they got ready to fight back.

A Jewish priest and his five sons led the rebels. One son, Judah Maccabeus, was the main leader. The Jewish soldiers were called the Maccabees. The Maccabees used their knowledge of the land against the stronger

Syrian forces. They won battle after battle. By 164 B.C., the Maccabees had gained control of Jerusalem.

1. What caused the Jews to rebel against Syrian rule?

_____

_____

_____

_____

Roman Control

(pages 344–345)

What was the result of Jewish resistance to Roman rule?

The Jews briefly ruled Judah again. However, in 63 B.C., the Romans conquered Judah. They called the land Judea. The Romans tightly controlled Judea. They appointed Jewish kings and religious leaders. Some Jews wanted to go along with Roman rule. Others wanted to free Judea.

READING STUDY GUIDE

READING STUDY GUIDE CONTINUED

In A.D. 66, a group of Jews called the Zealots made attacks on Roman troops. The Romans sent Vespasian, a general, to crush the uprising. Some Jews feared he would destroy the Temple. A teacher named Yohanan ben Zaccai went to the Roman leader. He asked Vespasian to set aside a place for Jews to study. This school kept alive Jewish traditions.

Vespasian put his son Titus in charge of Roman troops in Judea. In A.D. 70, Titus put down the rebellion. He also took Jerusalem and burned the Second Temple. Some Zealots kept fighting at a fortress called Masada, but it was taken.

The destruction of the Second Temple and the capture of Jerusalem, hastened the scattering of the Jews from their homeland. This scattering, which had begun peacefully centuries earlier, is called the **Diaspora.** They went to many other parts of the world. Many Jews were taken as slaves to Rome. However, some Jews stayed in Jerusalem, too.

2. How did the Romans react to Jewish rebellion?

_____

_____

_____

_____

_____

Judaism—An Ongoing Faith

(pages 345–346)

What happened to Jewish beliefs in exile?

The Jews were scattered throughout the Roman Empire. However, many stayed faithful to their beliefs.

After the Second Temple was destroyed, many Jews worried that they would lose their identity. Religious leaders and teachers called **rabbis** worked to keep this from happening. Wherever Jews settled they built **synagogues.** These are places for Jews to worship. There, people came to listen to rabbis read the Torah. They also read interpretations of the Torah called the Commentaries.

The Jews also kept their faith by carefully following their laws and customs. They built schools where their children could study the Torah and learn prayers.

3. How did the Jews preserve their ways of life?

_____

_____

_____

_____

_____

READING STUDY GUIDE

CHAPTER 10 The Hebrew Kingdoms

Chapter 10 The Hebrew Kingdoms

Glossary/After You Read

appoint to choose for an office, position, or duty

dispute an argument or quarrel

faithful loyal; devoted

fame great reputation; public esteem; renown

observe to follow or do properly

outcome result

promise to pledge to do something

shepherd a person who tends to sheep

sustain to support the spirits of

threat a possible danger

Terms & Names

A. If the statement is true, write "true" on the line. If it is false, change the underlined words to make it true.

_____ **1.** The belief in one god is called <u>monotheism</u>.

_____ **2.** A <u>priest</u> is a spiritual leader who can interpret God's word.

_____ **3.** A Jewish religious leader and teacher is called a <u>minister</u>.

_____ **4.** Jews worship in a building called a <u>synagogue</u>.

_____ **5.** Throughout history some Jews have hoped that God would send a chosen leader, called the <u>Messiah</u>.

B. Write the letter of the name or term that best matches the description.

_____ **6.** The leader who made Jerusalem the capital of Israel

_____ **7.** The father of the Hebrews

_____ **8.** The migration of the Hebrews out of Egypt

_____ **9.** The laws the Hebrews received from God

_____ **10.** The religion of the Jews

a. Ten Commandments

b. David

c. Abraham

d. Judaism

e. Exodus

f. Diaspora

READING STUDY GUIDE

Main Ideas

11. How did Judaism start?

_____

_____

12. According to the Torah, where did the Ten Commandments come from?

_____

_____

13. What were some of Solomon's achievements?

_____

_____

14. What was the Babylonian Captivity?

_____

_____

15. What hastened the Diaspora?

_____

_____

Thinking Critically

16. Understanding Cause and Effect How do you think the Hebrews' history affected their beliefs?

_____

_____

_____

17. Making Inferences Why do you think the Ten Commandments are still important today?

_____

_____

_____

CHAPTER 11 | LESSON 1 The Geography of Greece

Lesson 1 The Geography of Greece

BEFORE YOU READ

In Lesson 1, you will learn how geography affected the development of the Greek civilization.

AS YOU READ

Use this chart to take notes about how geography affected ancient Greece.

Causes	Effects
Mountains cover most of Greece.	
Several seas surround Greece.	
Greece traded with other regions.	

TERMS & NAMES

- **Peninsula** a body of land that has water on three sides
- **Peloponnesus** the southern peninsula of Greece
- **isthmus** a narrow strip of land connecting two larger bodies of land
- **Phoenicians** a group of trading people on the coast of the eastern Mediterranean
- **alphabet** a system of symbols that stands for sounds

Geography Shapes Greek Life

(pages 355–356)

What were the main features of the geography of Greece?

Greece is a **peninsula,** or body of land that has water on three sides. The mainland of Greece borders the Mediterranean Sea. Thousands of islands also make up Greece.

The Greek peninsula is divided in two. The **Peloponnesus** is the southern peninsula. An **isthmus,** or narrow strip of land, joins the Peloponnesus to the rest of Greece.

Most of Greece is made up of mountains. The mountains divide Greece into many rugged regions. They make transportation difficult. There are no rivers in Greece for travel. The rugged landscape made it difficult to bring Greece together under one government.

Greece has a warm climate. This kind of climate led to an outdoor life for the Greek people.

Because the land in Greece is rocky, very little of it could be used for farming. But most Greeks were farmers or herders. In Greece, landowners made up the upper class. Landowners could support themselves. They also had enough money to buy helmets and weapons. As a result, landowners could serve in the army and defend their land.

To get more farmland, the Greeks found colonies in other places. They set up many colonies in Anatolia, which had plains and rivers.

Greece also did not have enough natural resources such as metals. They had to get these resources from someplace else. Greece did have stone for building. It also had good places for harbors.

1. Why did Greeks set up colonies?

_____

_____

_____

_____

READING STUDY GUIDE

Trade Helped Greece Prosper

(page 357)

How did the sea affect Greek life?

The sea was important to Greece. On the south is the Mediterranean Sea. The Ionian Sea is west of Greece, and the Aegean Sea is east. These seas linked the different parts of Greece to each other. The seas were important for transportation.

The Greeks were skilled sailors. They also were skilled ship builders. They built rowing ships for fighting and trading. The sea also provided the Greeks with fish, an important part of the Greek diet. The Greeks traded fish for other products.

The Greeks did not grow much grain. They did produce olive oil, wine, wool, and pottery. Greek city-states bought and sold these products from each other. Greeks also traded these products with places such as Egypt and Italy. The Greeks bought products such as grain, timber, flax to make linen, and slaves.

2. How was fish important to the Greeks?

_____

_____

_____

_____

The Earliest Greeks

(pages 358–359)

How did trade influence Greek culture?

The earliest people had moved into Greece by about 2000 B.C. The first Greek civilization started on the Peloponnesus. It was named after its most important city, Mycenae. A king ruled each Mycenaean city. The people were traders. Their culture had writing, gold jewelry, and bronze weapons. By 1200 B.C., the Mycenaean civilization disappeared. Between 1200 and 700 B.C., Greek culture declined. During this time, people did not keep written records. As a result, historians know very little about the decline of this culture.

In time, Greek culture began to advance again. This is because the Greeks began to learn from other people. One group they learned from was the **Phoenicians,** a trading people. The Phoenicians lived on the coast of the eastern Mediterranean. The Greeks picked up the alphabet from the Phoenicians. This was a system of writing in which 22 symbols stood for sound. Eventually, the Greek **alphabet** became the alphabet we use today. The Greeks learned about making coins from people in Anatolia. The Anatolians invented coins.

3. What did the Greeks learn from the Phoenicians?

_____

_____

_____

_____

CHAPTER 11 | LESSON 2 Beliefs and Customs

Lesson 2 Beliefs and Customs

BEFORE YOU READ

In Lesson 2, you will learn about Greek religion, Greek customs, and Greek literature.

AS YOU READ

Use this chart to show how Greek beliefs were related to Greek literature..

Greek Beliefs	Greek Literature

TERMS & NAMES

• **Zeus** the ruler of the Greek gods
• **Mount Olympus** the highest mountain in Greece and home to the Greek gods
• **myth** stories that people tell to explain beliefs about their world
• **Olympics** games held every four years in Greece
• **epic poem** long poems that told stories
• **fable** a short story that teaches a moral lesson

Greek Gods and Myths

(pages 361–362)

What was Greek religion like?

The Greeks worshiped many gods. The gods had both godlike and human qualities. They were not always nice. **Zeus** was the ruler of the gods. Greeks believed that he and 11 other gods lived on **Mount Olympus,** the highest mountain in Greece. In addition to these 12 gods, the Greeks worshiped many lesser gods. Each Greek city-state had a special god who protected it. For example, Athena was the goddess of Athens.

The Greeks created **myths** to explain how the world and people were created. Myths are stories that explain people's beliefs about their world. Many myths described Greek gods and goddesses. Some myths told about Greek heroes and heroines.

1. Why did the Greeks create myths?

_____

_____

_____

_____

Honoring the Gods

(pages 362–363)

How did the Greeks honor their gods?

The Greeks believed it was important to honor and worship the gods. They believed that not doing so could cause gods to be angry and bring trouble on the Greeks. Certain days were holy to certain gods and goddesses. The Greeks celebrated these days with sacrifices and festivals. The most important festivals honored the 12 most important Greek gods.

Religious festivals always included games. The **Olympics** were the largest of these games and they honored Zeus. The Olympics took place every four years. Only men took part in the Olympic games.

READING STUDY GUIDE

READING STUDY GUIDE CONTINUED

2. Which god did the Olympic games honor?

_____

_____

_____

_____

Early Greek Literature

(pages 364–365)

What literature did the early Greeks produce?
The Greeks told stories about their heroes. Many of these stories were long poems called **epic poems.** They tell us much about the early Greeks.

A man named Homer wrote the most famous epics. His epic about the Trojan War is called the *Iliad*. During this story, the Greeks surrounded the city of Troy for almost 10 years to try to capture it. The *Iliad* is famous for what it told about Greek heroes. For hundreds of years, people thought that the story was fiction. But around 1870, archaeologists found the ruins of ancient Troy. But the real Trojan War did not happen in the same way as the Iliad describes it.

Another epic poem by Homer was the *Odyssey*. It tells about the Greek hero Odysseus and his adventures after the Trojan War. The *Odyssey* tells about the dangers that Odysseus faced in the ten years it took him to get home.

A Greek storyteller named Aesop wrote many Greek fables. A **fable** is a short story that teaches a moral lesson. The stories usually involve animals. One of Aesop's best-known fables is "The Hare and the Tortoise."

3. What are the *Iliad* and the *Odyssey* about?

_____

_____

_____

_____

READING STUDY GUIDE

CHAPTER 11 | LESSON 3 The City-State and Democracy

Lesson 3 The City-State and Democracy

BEFORE YOU READ

In Lesson 3, you will learn what types of government developed in ancient Greece.

AS YOU READ

Use this chart to take notes about the types of government that existed in ancient Greece.

Types of Government			
Monarchy	Aristocracy	Oligarchy	Democracy

TERMS & NAMES

- **polis** the Greek word for city-state
- **aristocracy** a government in which the upper class rules
- **oligarchy** a government in which a small group rules
- **tyrant** someone who took power in an illegal way
- **citizen** a person who is loyal to a government and is entitled to protection by the government
- **democracy** a government in which the citizens make political decisions

The Rise of City-States

(pages 371–372)

How was Greece organized politically?

Because geography separated Greece into small regions, the main form of government in Greece was the city-state. A city-state is a city that rules its surrounding farmlands. The Greek word for city-state was **polis.** The largest Greek city-states were Sparta and Athens.

Most city-states in Greece had fewer than 20,000 people. Because a city-state was small, the people who lived there formed a close community. The center of the city was the agora. This was an open space where people met to do business and to talk about politics. Festivals were also held at the agora.

Many cities had an acropolis. This was a hilltop that was protected against attack. The acropolis was first used for military purposes. Later, Greeks built temples on the flat tops of the hills. Regular houses were built on the bottom of the hill.

1. What was the acropolis used for?

_____

_____

_____

_____

Forms of Government

(pages 372–373)

What different political systems evolved in the city-states of Greece?

Each city-state had its own kind of government. Some city-states kept the same kind of government for a long time. In other city-states, the government changed from one system to another.

The earliest kind of government in Greece was a monarchy. This is a kind of government in which a monarch rules. A monarch is a king or queen who has supreme power. In some city-states, a monarchy gave way to a government called an aristocracy. An

READING STUDY GUIDE

aristocracy is a government in which the upper class rules.

Some city-states developed an **oligarchy.** This is a government in which a few people control the government. What is the difference between an oligarchy and an aristocracy? In an aristocracy, people rule because of their inherited social class. In an oligarchy, people rule because they are wealthy or landowners.

Poor people in Greece were often not part of government. They often resented this and sometimes rebelled. Sometimes a wealthy person who wanted power asked poor people to support him in becoming a leader. Such leaders were called tyrants. In Greece, a **tyrant** was a person who took power in an illegal way. Some Greek tyrants worked to help the poor.

2. How did tyrants often come to power?

_____

_____

_____

_____

Athens Builds a Limited Democracy

(pages 374–376)

How did limited democracy develop in Athens?
In time, people in the lower classes realized that they could influence government. They began to demand more power.

The Greeks invented the idea of citizenship. Today, a **citizen** is a person who is loyal to a government and who is entitled to protection by the government. In Greece, a citizen was a person who had the right to take part in ruling the city-state. To be a citizen, a person had to be born to free citizens.

In the 500s B.C., two leaders made reforms that gave people more power. These leaders were Solon and Cleisthenes. In Athens, many poor people owed more money than they could repay. Because of this, they were forced to become slaves. As a result, people in the lower

classes grew angry with their rulers.

In 594 B.C., Solon was elected to lead Athens. He freed people who were forced to become slaves because of debt. He made a law that no citizens could be made slaves. Solon organized citizens into four classes that were based on wealth. All citizens were allowed to be part of the assembly and help elect leaders.

Cleisthenes increased the citizens' power even more. He took power away from the nobles. He organized citizens into groups based on where they lived. Any citizen could vote on laws.

Athens government became a form of **democracy.** This is a government in which the citizens make political decisions. Athens had a direct democracy. All citizens met to decide on the laws. Athens also had a limited democracy. Only free adult males were citizens who could take part in the government. Women, slaves, and foreigners could not take part. People who were not citizens were not allowed to become citizens.

3. How did Cleisthenes' reforms give people more power?

_____

_____

_____

_____

Lesson 4 Sparta and Athens

BEFORE YOU READ

In Lesson 4, you will learn what life was like in Sparta and Athens.

AS YOU READ

Use this diagram to tell how life in Sparta and Athens was the same and how it was different.

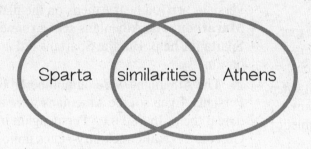

Sparta | similarities | Athens

TERMS & NAMES

- **Athens** a large city-state in the Peloponnesus
- **Sparta** a large city-state in the Peloponnesus
- **helot** a slave in Sparta
- **barracks** military houses in Sparta
- **Marathon** a plain near Athens and site of a battle in the Persian Wars

Sparta's Military State

(pages 379–380)

What did Spartan society emphasize the most?

The main rival of **Athens** was **Sparta.** About 715 B.C., Sparta began to conquer nearby areas to get land. Sparta forced many of the people it defeated to become slaves called **helots.** Helots worked on farms. They had to give the Spartans half their crops. The Helots outnumbered the Spartans. They hated Spartan rule and rebelled many times. The Spartans put down these revolts. But the Spartans also feared Helot revolts. Because of this, they stressed building a strong army.

Two kings ruled Sparta. Five elected supervisors ran the government. Thirty older citizens made up the Council of Elders. They proposed laws. An Assembly voted on the suggested laws of the Council. This Assembly was made up of all Spartan citizens.

Sparta had three social groups. Citizens lived in the city. They spent all their time training to be soldiers. Free noncitizens lived in nearby villages. They had no political rights. The lowest group was the helots.

The goal of Spartans was to have a strong army. At age seven, boys moved into military houses called **barracks.** The boys' education focused on military skill. All male citizens joined the army when they were 20 years old. They stayed in the army until they were 60.

Spartan women were expected to be tough. Girls were educated to be strong and to defend themselves. For Spartans, the army was more important than family life. Because of this, husbands and wives spent much time apart. Women had some rights, such as being able to own property.

1. How was Sparta's society organized?

_____

_____

_____

_____

_____

READING STUDY GUIDE CONTINUED

Athens' Democratic Way of Life

(page 381)

What was the government of Athens like?

Athens had a direct democracy. All citizens met to vote on laws. The government of Athens included the Council of Four Hundred and the Assembly. The Council took care of day-to-day problems. The Assembly voted on laws suggested by the Council. Citizens in Athens served in the army whenever they were needed. Citizens also served on juries.

In Athens, citizens were organized into four classes that were based on wealth. Foreigners, women, children, and slaves were not citizens.

Boys of wealthy families started school when they were seven years old. They studied many different subjects. They also took part in athletic activities.

Women in Athens were expected to keep the family strong. They could inherit property only if the family had no sons. Girls did not go to school. They learned how to do household chores from their mothers.

2. Who was allowed to vote on laws in Athens?

_____

_____

_____

The Persian Wars

(pages 382–383)

What happened when Persia invaded Greece?

In the 500s B.C., Persia conquered Anatolia, which had many Greek colonies. In 499 B.C., some Greeks in Anatolia rebelled against the Persians. Athens sent soldiers and ships to help these Greeks. After the revolt failed, the Persians decided to punish Athens for helping the Greek colonists. Around 490 B.C., the Persians arrived near Athens on the plain of **Marathon.** The Athenians sent a runner to ask Sparta for help. But the Spartans did not arrive on time.

The Athenians were outnumbered by the Persians. Even so, the Athenians were able to defeat them. In 480 B.C., Persia again invaded Greece. Several Greek city-states united to fight and eventually defeated the Persians.

3. Why did the Persians attack Athens around 490 B.C.?

_____

_____

_____

_____

READING STUDY GUIDE

Chapter 11 Ancient Greece

Glossary/After You Read

bodies groups acting together

clever smart; showing quick thinking and resourcefulness

entitled having rights and privileges

found establish; bring into being

hero a person who is admired for great courage or special achievements

mainland the main part of a country or territory

proposed suggested, put forward for consideration

rugged having a rough, jagged, or uneven surface

Terms & Names

A. Write the letter of the term that best completes each sentence.

_____ 1. A(n) _____ connected the Peloponnesus with the rest of Greece.

_____ 2. The Phoenicians were the first people to develop a(n) _____.

_____ 3. Greek _____ told of gods, goddesses, heroes, and heroines.

_____ 4. The Greek word for city-state was _____.

_____ 5. The government in Athens was a direct _____.

a. polis
b. democracy
c. myths
d. isthmus
e. alphabet
f. fables

B. In the blank, write the letter of the choice that best completes the statement or answers the question.

_____ 6. Most of Greece is covered by _____.

a. deserts　　b. plains　　c. mountains　　d. isthmuses

_____ 7. In order to get more farmland, the Greeks _____.

a. set up colonies　　b. irrigated their land　　c. farmed on the mountainsides　　d. farmed in England

_____ 8. The _____ civilization was the first Greek civilization.

a. Persian　　b. Spartan　　c. Athenian　　d. Mycenaean

_____ 9. The Iliad and the Odyssey are two famous Greek _____.

a. fables　　b. epic poems　　c. myths　　d. festivals

_____ 10. A government in which the upper class rules is a(n) _____.

a. aristocracy　　b. oligarchy　　c. monarchy　　d. democracy

READING STUDY GUIDE

Main Ideas

11. How were the seas important to the Greeks?

_____

_____

12. How did Greeks honor their gods?

_____

_____

13. What were two types of early Greek literature and what were they about?

_____

_____

14. How was an aristocracy different than an oligarchy?

_____

_____

15. How was education in Sparta different than education in Athens?

_____

_____

Thinking Critically

16. Understanding Cause and Effect How did geography affect the development of Greece?

_____

_____

17. Forming and Supporting Opinions Would you rather have lived in Sparta or in Athens? Explain why.

_____

_____

CHAPTER 12 | LESSON 1 The Golden Age of Greece

Lesson 1 The Golden Age of Greece

BEFORE YOU READ

In this lesson, you will read about a time of high achievement in ancient Greece.

AS YOU READ

Use this graphic organizer to record three of Pericles' goals and details about each.

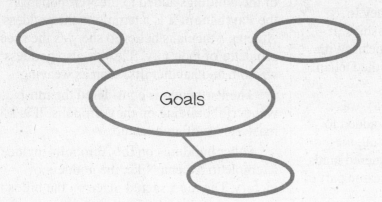

Goals

TERMS & NAMES

- **Pericles** A great leader of Athens
- **direct democracy** A system in which all citizens take part in running the government
- **Delian League** A group of Greek city-states who united for defense
- **Acropolis** A high section of Athens where important buildings are located
- **Parthenon** The main temple to the goddess Athena

Pericles Leads Athens

(pages 393–394)

What democratic changes did Pericles make?

Pericles was one of Athens' greatest leaders. He took control in 461 B.C. and led the city until his death 32 years later. This time in Athens is often called the Age of Pericles.

Pericles had three goals for Athens. He wanted to strengthen democracy. He wanted to expand Athens' empire. He wanted to make the city more beautiful.

Leaders in Athens had already started to expand democracy. Pericles supported these changes. However, he wanted to improve the balance of power between rich and poor.

In 430 B.C., Pericles gave a speech to honor Athenian soldiers. "Everyone is equal before the law," he said. It does not matter what class a person belongs to. What matters is the person's ability.

To spread power more fairly, Pericles changed the rule for holding public office. Most public officials served without pay. This meant that only wealthy people could afford

to do it. Pericles increased the number of paid positions. Now even poor citizens could hold public office. However, only free males over 18 years old, whose parents were both born in Athens, were citizens.

Democracy in Athens was different from democracy in the United States today. Athens was a **direct democracy**. All citizens took part in running the government. For example, all citizens could suggest and vote for laws themselves. The United States is a representative democracy. U.S. citizens elect other citizens to run the government. The representatives suggest and vote on laws for the citizens.

1. How did Pericles change the government of Athens?

   _____

   _____

   _____

   _____

Expanding the Empire

(page 395)

How did Athens become more powerful?

Greek wealth depended on overseas trade. Athens wanted to protect this. After the Persian War, the city organized a *league* with other city-states for defense. It was called the **Delian League.** It was called this because its first headquarters was on the island of Delos.

Pericles used the League's money to build a navy. The fleet had 200 warships. It was the strongest in the Mediterranean. With this power, Athens took control of the Delian League.

In 454 B.C., the League's treasury was moved from Delos to Athens. This added to Athens' power. Athens started treating the other member city-states like conquered lands. Eventually, the other city-states became part of an Athenian empire.

2. How did Athens' power grow?

_____

_____

_____

_____

Beautifying Athens

(pages 396–397)

How did Pericles beautify Athens?

After the Persian War, Athens was in ruins. Pericles thought that this was a chance to rebuild, *glorify*, and beautify Athens.

The Greek city-states paid a tribute to the Delian League's treasury. The money was supposed to build the power of the League. Instead, Pericles used the money to make Athens beautiful again. He did not ask approval from the other members of the League. His action angered the other city-states.

Pericles spent the money on gold, ivory, and marble. These were used to make sculptures and beautiful buildings in Athens. Pericles also used the money to pay the artists, architects, and sculptors who worked on these projects.

One of the areas that needed to be rebuilt was the **Acropolis.** It is a hill in Athens where important buildings are located. One of the buildings added to the Acropolis was the **Parthenon.** It is a temple to the goddess Athena. Athenians believed she was the special protector of their city. She was also goddess of wisdom and handicrafts, such as weaving.

The Parthenon is considered the most wonderful building on the Acropolis. It is a masterpiece of architecture.

Other buildings on the Acropolis include a temple to Athena Nike, the goddess of victory. The most sacred place on the hill is the Erechtheum. It is considered the most perfect example of a Greek building. Legend says it marks the spot where Athena had a contest with the god Poseidon to see who would be the god of the city. Athena won.

3. What did Pericles do to make Athens beautiful?

_____

_____

_____

_____

READING STUDY GUIDE

Lesson 2 Peloponnesian War

BEFORE YOU READ

In this lesson, you will read about a war among the Greek city-states.

AS YOU READ

Use this graphic organizer to take notes about the different ways Sparta and Athens fought.

War Strategy	
Athens	Sparta

TERMS & NAMES

- **Peloponnesian War** The war between Athens and Sparta
- **plague** A an easily spread disease that usually causes death
- **truce** An agreement to stop fighting

The Outbreak of War

(pages 399–400)

What led Athens and Sparta to fight a war?

For years tension had been building between the city-states Sparta and Athens. Now Sparta did not like that Athens was so powerful.

The two city-states were very different. For example, Athens was a democracy. Sparta glorified military ideals. However, both wanted to be the most powerful city-state in Greece. This rivalry led to clashes between the two city-states and their *allies*.

War broke out for three main reasons. First, some city-states feared Athens. They did not like its grab for power and *prestige*. Second, under Pericles, Athens grew from a city-state to a naval empire. Third, some Athenians began to settle on lands belonging to other city-states.

The other city-states also disliked how Athens had spent the Delian League's money on itself. The money was supposed to be for mutual protection. Athens had used it to beautify Athens. Because of this, several city-states tried to break free. Pericles punished any city-state that resisted Athenian control.

The city-states that were angry with Athens formed their own league. It was led by Sparta and was called the Peloponnesian League. This was because many of the members were on the Peloponnesian peninsula. Finally, in 431 B.C. Sparta declared war on Athens. This war was the **Peloponnesian War.**

1. Why did Sparta and Athens go to war?

_____

_____

_____

_____

READING STUDY GUIDE CONTINUED

The War Rages

(pages 400–401)

What happened during the Peloponnesian War?

Each side in the war had strengths. Sparta had the best army. It could also not be attacked by sea. Athens had the best navy. It could use the navy to go after Sparta's allies, if not Sparta. The differences shaped the war *strategies* of each side.

Sparta's plan was to destroy Athenian crops and starve the city. The Spartans did this by taking control of the *countryside* around Athens.

Athens' plan was to avoid land battles and rely on their navy. Pericles persuaded the Athenians to let the Spartans destroy the countryside. He brought the people inside the walls of Athens. The idea was that they would all be safe. Food could be brought to the city by sea.

Unfortunately, Athens became overcrowded. In the second year of the war, a plague broke out. A **plague** is a killer disease that spreads easily. About one third of the Athenian people died. This included Pericles. In 421 B.C., Athens signed a **truce** to stop the fighting for a while. Athens finally surrendered to Sparta in 404 B.C.

2. What happened to weaken Athens during the war?

_____

_____

_____

_____

Consequences of the War

(page 402)

What was the result of the Peloponnesian War?

The Peloponnesian War lasted more than 25 years. Cities and crops were ruined. Thousands of Greeks died. All city-states lost economic and military power. It was not something that they would recover from quickly.

In the north, Philip of Macedonia would come to power in 359 B.C. Dreaming of building an empire, he would look south to the weakened Greek city-states.

3. What did the Peloponnesian War do to the city-states?

_____

_____

_____

_____

READING STUDY GUIDE

CHAPTER 12 | LESSON 3 Alexander the Great

Lesson 3 Alexander the Great

BEFORE YOU READ

In this lesson, you will read how Alexander the Great became one of the most successful military leaders in history.

AS YOU READ

Use this chart to take notes about the effects of the conditions listed.

Causes	Effects
Weak governments	
New weapons of warfare	
Foreign conquests	

TERMS & NAMES

- **catapult** A military machine that hurls objects
- **Alexander the Great** A great military leader of Macedonia who conquered a huge empire
- **Hellenistic** Describes a cultural blend of Greek, Egyptian, Persian, and Indian styles
- **Alexandria** Alexander's capital in Egypt and the most famous Hellenistic city

The Kingdom of Macedonia

(pages 405–406)

Who conquered the Greek city-states?

While the Greek city-states were fighting, a new power was growing to the north. This was Macedonia. Its king, Philip, was 23 years old and had plans to build an empire.

As a teenager, Philip had been a hostage in the city-state of Thebes. There he learned about its army and strategies. From this experience, Philip saw that a professional army might be better than one made up of citizen-soldiers.

When he became king, he built a professional army. He thought up new battle formations and tactics. He tried different combinations of cavalry and foot soldiers. He gave his men new weapons. One of these was a catapult for hurling objects at city walls. His soldiers also used battering rams.

After conquering the lands around Macedonia, Philip turned to the Greek city-states. By 338 b.c., he ruled them all. Because he respected Greek ways, he did not destroy

Athens. He took Greeks into his army and got ready to fight Persia.

However, in 336 b.c. Philip was murdered. His 20-year-old son, Alexander, took the throne.

1. Why was Philip able to attack the Greek city-states?

_____

_____

Alexander Tries to Conquer the World

(pages 406–407)

How did Alexander build an empire?

Alexander was well trained to be king. The best Greek scholars had *tutored* him. He had trained in his father's army, too. He picked up his father's plans.

Before he could attack Persia, however, Thebes rebelled. Alexander destroyed the city. This cruel punishment made the other Greek

READING STUDY GUIDE

city-states afraid to rebel. Then Alexander moved his troops to Anatolia. There he attacked Persian forces. He defeated them through bold tactics.

Next, Alexander turned south to Egypt, which was ruled by the Persians. The Egyptians welcomed Alexander. They hated the Persians. They even made Alexander the pharaoh.

After taking over Egypt, Alexander moved across Mesopotamia toward Persia. Finally he conquered the Persian capital, Persepolis. By 331 B.C., Alexander controlled the Persian Empire.

In the next three years, Alexander conquered parts of Central Asia. In 326 B.C., he reached the Indus River Valley and India. Alexander wanted to continue east, but his armies refused. They had been fighting for 11 years and were thousands of miles from home. Alexander was forced to turn back.

In 323 B.C., Alexander and his armies had reached Babylon. While there, Alexander fell ill and died. He was 32 years old. However, he had conquered a huge empire. Because of his accomplishments, he is called Alexander the Great.

Alexander had not had time to unite his empire. There was fighting among his generals after his death. None of them was strong enough to rule the whole empire. Eventually, it was divided among the three most powerful generals.

2. What older empire did Alexander defeat?

_____

_____

The Legacy of Alexander

(pages 408–409)

How did culture change under Alexander's rule?

Alexander and his armies brought their culture everywhere they went. In his new lands, Alexander set up colonies. He built cities based on Greek ideas. He named as many as 70 of them Alexandria, after himself.

Alexander left Greeks behind to rule his lands. Greek became the common language under his rule. At the same time, Alexander took on Persian clothing styles. He adopted Persian customs. He urged his soldiers to do the same. Some Greek colonists married Persians and took on Persian ways. In Egypt, the Greek rulers blended Egyptian culture with Greek styles. In India the same thing happened.

This blend of Greek, Persian, Egyptian, and Indian ways became known as **Hellenistic** culture. It influenced the lands in the empire for hundreds of years.

Learning was especially affected. Greek, Egyptian, Arab, and Indian scholars shared information. They studied together. Their combined knowledge made new discoveries possible in science and medicine.

The most famous Hellenistic city was Alexandria. Alexander founded it in Egypt in 332 B.C. The city was an important center of learning for over 500 years. The library there contained major collections of Greek and non-Greek texts. Scholars came from the Mediterranean area and Asia to study there.

Also in Alexandria was the Temple of the Muses. Muses are goddesses who rule the arts and sciences. Many examples of the arts and sciences were stored there. Today we would call it a *museum,* after the Muses. Alexandria also boasted a huge lighthouse. Its light could be seen from 35 miles away. It was one of the Seven Wonders of the Ancient World.

3. How did Alexander's conquests affect science and other areas of knowledge?

_____

_____

Lesson 4 The Legacy of Greece

BEFORE YOU READ

In this lesson, you will read about the lasting contributions of classical Greece.

AS YOU READ

Use this diagram to take record details about the Greek and Hellenistic legacy.

The Arts & Architecture	History & Philosophy	Science & Technology

TERMS & NAMES

- **drama** A written work for actors to perform
- **tragedy** A serious drama that presents the downfall of an important character
- **comedy** A less serious drama that usually ends happily
- **ideal** A perfect form
- **philosophy** The study of basic truths of the universe

The Arts and Architecture

(pages 411–413)

What new features did the Greeks introduce in art and architecture?

The Greeks made many important contributions to western culture. For example, they invented drama. **Drama** is a work written for actors to perform.

Greek drama was part of each city's religious festival. Wealthy citizens would *sponsor* a production. Plays were submitted to the city's leader. He chose the ones he liked best. Then a play was assigned to a *troupe* of actors to perform. Prizes were given to the best writers.

There are two forms of drama: tragedy and comedy. **Tragedy** is a serious story. Usually it involves the downfall of an important character. Tragedies are often about love, war, and hate. One example of a tragedy is *Oedipus Rex* by Sophocles. In this play, a good man named Oedipus kills another man. Later, Oedipus finds out that the man was his father.

The second kind of drama is comedy. A **comedy** is a less serious story. Greek comedies often make fun of politics, important people, or ideas of that time. Comedies also have happy endings. Aristophanes was a great writer of comedies. One of his plays is the *Birds*. It makes fun of people who want power.

The Greeks also created great sculptures. Greek sculptors aimed to capture the **ideal** in their work. This means that they tried to create as perfect a form as possible. They wanted to create a sense of order, beauty, and harmony in all things.

Greek architects designed many buildings. These include temples, theaters, meeting places, and grand homes. Like the sculptors, the architects tried to design buildings with ideal *proportions*. Several specific features appear in Greek architecture. One of these is the column.

1. What did Greek artists try to create in their works?

_____

_____

History, Philosophy, and Democracy

(pages 414–415)

How did the Greek love of reason and logic influence the development of western knowledge?

Direct democracy was the form of government in many Greek city-states. Although not

everyone could be a citizen, for the first time those who were had a say in government. Greek ideas about government have been copied in many places over time. Democracy is still a goal for many nations.

The Greeks were also among the first people to write down their history. They did not just tell stories about the past. They analyzed what happened. They tried to understand the facts.

Herodotus was born in 484 B.C. He is sometimes called "the father of history." He wrote the history of the Persian War. Thucydides was an important Greek historian. He wrote a history of the Peloponnesian War. He supported what he wrote with documents and eyewitness accounts.

Greek thinkers began to question their values after the Peloponnesian War. From this questioning came philosophy. **Philosophy** is the study of basic truths and ideas about the world.

Greek philosophers had two main ideas about the world. First, they assumed that it was orderly and based on laws of nature. Second, they assumed that people could understand these laws. The philosophers used these two ideas in their thinking.

There were many famous philosophers in ancient Greece. One of them was Socrates. He lived from 470 to 399 B.C. Socrates encouraged his students to examine their beliefs. He did this by asking them a series of questions. This style of teaching is called the Socratic method.

One of Socrates' best students was Plato. He was born about 427 B.C. Plato wrote about an ideal government in a book called *The Republic*. His ideal was not a democracy. Instead, he believed that a wise philosopher-king should rule. Plato started an important school called the Academy. It stayed open for about 900 years.

Aristotle was Plato's best student. He lived from 384 to 322 B.C. Aristotle invented a way of debating. It followed rules of logic. Later, the rules were applied in scientific work. Aristotle had his own school called the Lyceum. In addition to his great works, Aristotle spent three years as a tutor to Alexander the Great.

2. What two ideas did Greek philosophers have about the universe?

_____

_____

Science and Technology

(pages 416–417)

Why is Hellenistic science so important?
Hellenistic scholars saved and added to the knowledge of Greek, Egyptian, and Indian thinkers.

Scientists at Alexandria made important discoveries in astronomy. For example, Eratosthenes closely estimated the distance around the earth. Aristarchus was another scientist in Alexandria. He studied how the sun, moon, and the earth relate to each other. He estimated the size of the sun, too. Ptolemy studied the solar system. He put the earth at its center. Unfortunately, people believed this mistake for the next 1,400 years.

Very complicated mathematics is needed in astronomy. Hellenistic thinkers developed several kinds of mathematics. Euclid created a geometry text. Today, courses on geometry are still based on his work.

Archimedes worked in physics. He explained the law of the lever. He also invented a compound pulley. It is possible that he also developed a water-lifting device. It was to be used to water crops. Later, his ideas were used to make pumps and eventually to make a steam engine.

The first noted female mathematician was Hypatia. She was also an astronomer. She taught at Alexandria and wrote about Euclid and Ptolemy's works. Hypatia was also the leader of a movement based on the works of Plato.

3. What kinds of discoveries did Hellenistic scholars make?

_____

_____

READING STUDY GUIDE

Chapter 12 Classical Greece

Glossary/After You Read

ability a skill

ally a country that has joined with another for a special purpose

common shared

compound made up of or using more than one

countryside a rural or agricultural region, as opposed to the city

glorify to bring honor, praise, and admiration to someone or something

hostage a person held to make sure demands are met

ivory the material that forms the tusks of animals, such as elephants

league a group working together for a common purpose

prestige importance or high respect

proportion the pleasing arrangement of various parts of a whole in relation to each other

sponsor to support another person or thing

strategy a plan designed to reach a specific goal

style a way of dressing or behaving

troupe a group, especially of performers

tutor to give individual instruction

Terms & Names

A. Write the letter of the name or term that best completes each sentence.

_____ 1. Many Greek city-states had governments based on _____.

_____ 2. _____ conquered the Persian Empire.

_____ 3. A _____ is a type of war machine used by Philip of Macedonia.

_____ 4. The Athenians had to call a _____ with the Spartans to stop the war.

_____ 5. During the wars with Sparta, Athens was struck by a _____ that killed about one-third of its people.

a. catapult

b. direct democracy

c. plague

d. truce

e. Alexander the Great

f. Peloponnesian War

B. Write the letter of the name or term that best matches the description.

_____ 6. One of the greatest leaders of Athens

_____ 7. A temple to Athena

_____ 8. A center of learning in Egypt

_____ 9. The group formed by Greek city-states for defense

_____ 10. The hill in Athens that featured temples and other important buildings

a. Hellenistic

b. Pericles

c. Parthenon

d. Delian League

e. Alexandria

f. Acropolis

Main Ideas

11. What three improvements did Pericles want to make?

_____

_____

12. How did Athens build an empire?

_____

_____

13. The Peloponnesian War was fought mainly between what two city-states?

_____

14. How was Hellenistic culture created and spread?

_____

_____

_____

15. Who were three important Greek philosophers?

_____

Thinking Critically

16. Forming and Supporting Opinions Do you think Alexander was "the Great"? Why or why not?

_____

_____

17. Detecting Historical Points of View Why do you think leaders in Athens were so threatened by Socrates teachings?

_____

_____

Lesson 1 The Geography of Ancient Rome

BEFORE YOU READ

In this lesson, you will learn how geography influenced the development of the Roman civilization.

AS YOU READ

Use a web diagram like the one below to record information about Rome's beginnings, geography, and early people.

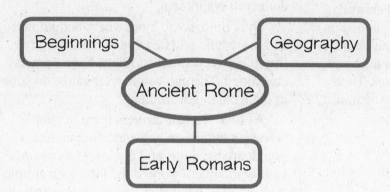

TERMS & NAMES
• **legend** a popular story from earlier times that cannot be proved
• **Aeneas** hero of the Trojan War who settled in Italy
• **Romulus** legendary hero and founder of Rome
• **Remus** Romulus' twin who helped found Rome
• **republic** a government in which people elect their leaders
• **peninsula** a piece of land surrounded on three sides by water

The Beginnings of Rome

(pages 431–432)

What is the early history of Rome?

A **legend** tells that Rome was founded in 753 B.C. A legend is a popular story from earlier times that cannot be proved. According to the legend, **Aeneas,** a hero of the Trojan War, settled in Italy after Troy was destroyed. His descendants, the twins **Romulus** and **Remus,** decided to found a city. However, they fought over its boundaries. Romulus killed his brother, and built the city around the Palatine Hill.

After Romulus, several Roman kings ruled the city. Around the 600s B.C., people known as Etruscans conquered Rome. In 509 B.C., the Romans overthrew the Etruscans and formed a **republic.** A republic is a government in which people elect their leaders.

1. What group of people conquered Rome around the 600s B.C.?

_____

_____

_____

READING STUDY GUIDE

READING STUDY GUIDE CONTINUED

Rome's Geographic Location

(pages 432–433)

Why was Rome's location so favorable?

The first settlers of Rome were really the Latins. They settled in Rome because it had a mild climate, good farmland, and a good location. The Latins founded Rome on seven hills. They farmed on land at the bottom of the hills. Rome's location near the Mediterranean Sea and the Tiber River encouraged trade.

Rome is located on the Italian Peninsula. A **peninsula** is a piece of land surrounded on three sides by water. Rome's position on the Mediterranean made it easier to conquer new territories and to develop trade routes. Two mountain ranges, the Alps and the Apennines, helped protect Rome from invasions.

2. Why did the Latins settle in Rome?

_____

_____

_____

_____

Lives of Early Romans

(pages 434–435)

What was life like for the early Romans?

Most early Romans were farmers. They grew grains such as wheat and barley and vegetables and fruit. Farmers who owned land also served in the army. For a time, only landowners were allowed to join the army. Roman leaders thought that only landowners would fight for the city. Landowners were also able to pay for their own equipment.

Over time, some landowners bought more and more land and became richer than others. A gap between small and large farm owners developed. The gap would later cause divisions in the Roman government.

At first, Roman farmers lived in simple homes in large family groups that included grandparents, aunts and uncles, and cousins. Family members worked the land with simple tools and fetched water from a well or spring. They had to grow enough food to feed the family.

3. How did most early Romans make a living?

_____

_____

_____

_____

Lesson 2 The Roman Republic

BEFORE YOU READ

In this lesson, you will learn about the society and government of the Roman Republic.

AS YOU READ

Use a chart like the one below to explain the effects of the events listed.

Causes	Effects
Romans no longer wanted a monarchy.	
Plebeians were not equal to the patricians.	
Rome expanded its territories.	

TERMS & NAMES

- **patrician** a member of the wealthy landowner class that held the highest positions in government
- **plebeian** a common farmer who could not hold important government positions
- **Senate** a powerful body of 300 members that advised Roman leaders
- **consul** a leader who led Rome's executive branch
- **Cincinnatus** Roman dictator who stepped down from power after one day

Early Strengths of Roman Society

(page 437)

How was Roman society structured?

Two social classes developed in Rome. The **patricians** were wealthy landowners who held all of the highest positions in government. The **plebeians** were mostly farmers. Plebeians could vote but could not hold important government positions.

The plebeians resented the patricians. In time, conflict developed between the two classes. Then around 450 b.c., patricians finally passed a set of laws called the Twelve Tables. These laws set up basic rights for all Roman citizens. They were the basis for all Roman law.

1. What were the Twelve Tables?

_____

_____

_____

_____

READING STUDY GUIDE CONTINUED

Republican Government

(pages 438–439)

How was the republican government organized?

The leaders of the Roman Republic set up a government with three branches. The legislative branch made the laws. Rome's legislative branch included the **Senate** and the assemblies. The Senate was made up of 300 members who advised Roman leaders. Most Senators were patricians. The assemblies were made up mostly of plebeians. They protected the rights of plebeians. The judicial branch ran the courts and governed the provinces. In Rome, the judicial branch was made up of eight judges.

The executive branch carried out the laws. Two **consuls** led Rome's executive branch. They directed the government for one year. Each consul was able to veto, or overrule, the other. In times of problems, the consuls chose a dictator to rule in their place. This was a leader with absolute power. The dictator was chosen to rule for a limited time. In 458 B.C., a man named **Cincinnatus** was made dictator to save Rome from an attack. He defeated the enemy and returned power to the consuls the same day.

The U.S. government is like the Roman government in many ways. The U.S. government has three branches of government. Each branch puts limits on the other so that no branch becomes too powerful. Like Rome, the United States has a written set of laws—the Constitution.

The Romans were proud to serve their nation, or perform their civic duty. Civic duty is also important in the United States today. People perform their civic duty by voting, paying taxes, and serving on a jury.

2. What was the role of the dictator in the Roman Republic?

_____

_____

_____

_____

The Republic Expands

(pages 440–441)

How did Rome expand?

After becoming a republic, Rome began expanding its territories. By 275 B.C., all of the Italian Peninsula was under Roman control. Rome offered citizenship to the people it conquered. It also allowed them to rule themselves. The conquered people had to pay taxes and send soldiers to the Roman army.

In 264 B.C., Rome began fighting the Punic Wars. These three wars were fought against the city of Carthage in North Africa. Rome won all three wars, although it almost lost the second. In 146 B.C., Rome captured and destroyed Carthage. The lands that Rome gained as a result of the wars extended Roman territory from Spain to Greece.

The Romans came back from the war with great wealth. They bought large farms and worked them using slaves. Many small farmers could not keep up with the large farmers, so they lost their land. Poverty increased, and the gap between rich and poor grew wider. This caused conflict between Rome's social classes.

3. What were the results of the Punic Wars?

_____

_____

_____

_____

READING STUDY GUIDE

Lesson 3 Rome Becomes an Empire

BEFORE YOU READ

In this lesson, you will learn what brought the Roman Republic to an end and how the Roman Empire began.

AS YOU READ

Use a time line like this one to keep track of the dates and events that led to the end of the Roman Republic and the beginning of the Roman Empire.

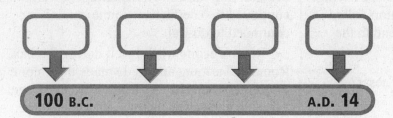

100 B.C.   A.D. 14

TERMS & NAMES

- **civil war** an armed conflict between groups within the same country
- **Julius Caesar** Roman general and dictator
- **Cicero** Roman consul and great speaker
- **Augustus** the first emperor of Rome
- **Pax Romana** a long period of peace and stability in Rome

Conflicts at Home

(pages 443–444)

What led to conflict in Rome?

As many wealthy people gained more power, the differences between rich and poor increased. The possibility of rebellions also grew. To help solve these problems, some reformers suggested breaking up the huge farms, or estates. They wanted to give some of the land to the poor. However, the wealthy landowners did not like these ideas and had the reformers killed.

At the same time, some powerful generals hired poor farmers to serve under them as soldiers. Soon these soldiers became more loyal to the generals than to the republic. Eventually, a **civil war** broke out. This is an armed conflict between groups within the same country. On one side were the generals backed by the plebeians. On the other were generals backed by patricians and senators. Finally after years of fighting, the patricians won, and a general named Sulla became a dictator.

1. What were the two groups that fought in the Roman civil war?

_____

_____

_____

Julius Caesar

(pages 444–446)

Who was Julius Caesar?

After Sulla died, other generals gained power. One of them was **Julius Caesar.** He proved to be a great general when he fought in Gaul, an area that is present-day France. Under Caesar, the Roman army defeated the Gauls and captured the entire area. The victory gave Rome more land and more wealth. It made Caesar famous and wealthy.

Caesar was also a good politician. He supported the common people, which made him popular with the plebeians. However, many powerful Romans were against Caesar. One of his opponents was **Cicero.** He was a Roman consul and an excellent speaker. Cicero did not trust Caesar or his desire for power.

READING STUDY GUIDE

When Caesar came back from Gaul, the Roman Senate ordered him to break up his army. Instead, Caesar led the army into Italy to fight for control of Rome. Caesar won and, when he returned to Rome in 46 B.C., the people and the army supported him. Then in 44 B.C., the Senate made Caesar dictator for life.

Caesar started many reforms. He expanded the Senate. He also created jobs for the poor. But some Romans feared that he would make himself king. Romans hated the idea of having a king. As a result, a group of senators killed Caesar in 44 B.C. This brought an end to the Roman Republic.

2. Why did some Romans fear Caesar?

_____

_____

_____

_____

Emperors Rule Rome

(pages 446–449)

What happened to Rome after Caesar's death?
After Caesar's death, a struggle for power took place among several Roman leaders. The struggle led to a civil war that lasted for years. Finally, in 27 B.C., Caesar's great-nephew and adopted son, Octavian, became the ruler of Rome. He took the name **Augustus,** which means "person of great rank and authority."

Augustus was the first emperor of Rome. He governed well. He brought the Roman provinces under control. He also started a civil service. This is a group of officials who work for the government. The Roman civil service collected taxes and took care of the postal system and the grain supply. Augustus also rebuilt Rome, making it more beautiful. He built large temples and theaters.

Under Augustus, Rome experienced a long time of peace. This time is called **Pax Romana,** or "Roman peace." It lasted about 200 years. During this time, Rome grew to its greatest size. Under Augustus, the Roman army was the biggest in the world. The army guarded the empire's borders. It also built roads, bridges, and tunnels. This helped link different places in the empire. Augustus also built a strong navy.

Many other leaders ruled after Augustus's death during the Pax Romana. The government continued to be effective, so the empire continued to do well.

Rome's economy did well during the Pax Romana. Farming and trade made the empire wealthy. Through trade, Rome was able to get valuable goods that it could not get at home. Traders traveled on trade routes that connected Rome with other parts of Europe and with parts of Africa and Asia.

A common currency, or money, was used throughout the empire, helping to unite it. The single currency made trade easier. Traders across the empire could buy and sell without changing their money into another currency.

3. What was the role of the army during the Pax Romana?

_____

_____

_____

_____

Lesson 4 The Daily Life of Romans

BEFORE YOU READ

In this lesson, you will learn about family life in Rome, Romans' religious beliefs, and life in Roman cities.

AS YOU READ

Use this web diagram to record some of the aspects of daily life of the Romans.

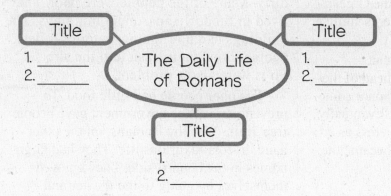

TERMS & NAMES
• **aqueduct** a system of channels and pipes used to carry fresh water from streams and lakes into towns
• **Colosseum** a Roman arena
• **gladiator** a trained warrior

Family and Society

(pages 453–454)

How were the family and society organized?

The father was the head of the Roman family. He owned all the property. He also had control over other members of the family. Roman women had more freedom than Greek women. They were expected to take care of the house and the children. Roman women could inherit property and could run businesses when their husbands were away. But women could not vote.

Most children received some education at home. Boys from wealthy families often attended private schools. Girls learned household skills at home.

Roman social classes changed over time. The patrician and plebeian classes turned into upper and lower classes. Patricians and some rich plebeians made up the upper class. A new middle class started. Business leaders and officials made up this class. Farmers were in one of the lower classes. However, slaves made up the lowest and largest class. Some slaves had low-level positions in government. But slaves did all the jobs that required physical labor. They worked in mines and farms. Many were treated harshly. Some slaves rebelled against their treatment.

1. Who had the most power in a Roman family?

_____

_____

Roman Beliefs

(pages 454–455)

What religious beliefs did the Romans hold?

Romans worshiped hundreds of spirits that they believed lived in everything around them. They also worshiped household gods that they believed protected them.

Other cultures also influenced Roman beliefs. The Romans borrowed the idea of gods in human form from the Etruscans. Many Roman gods were borrowed from the Greeks. For example, the Roman god Jupiter is similar to the Greek god Zeus.

In Rome, priests were government officials, and the emperor was the head of the church. Romans were expected to honor some of their gods in public ceremonies. Eventually, the Romans began to view the emperors as gods. Being loyal to the emperors became the same as being loyal to the gods.

2. What cultures influenced Roman beliefs?

_____

_____

Life in Roman Cities

(pages 456–458)

What was life like in Roman cities?

At the height of the Roman Empire, the city of Rome had almost 1 million people. It was the center of the empire. People from all over the empire came to live there. This resulted in a blend of ideas and customs.

The great number of people also caused Rome to be very crowded and dirty. Many of the people were poor. They lived in rundown apartment buildings. The buildings had no running water or toilets. People threw their trash into the street. Fires were also a problem.

The poor people had little food. To prevent unrest, the government gave people free grain. Wealthy Romans, on the other hand, lived a luxurious life. They had large homes in the countryside. They enjoyed themselves by going to the theater and holding large dinner parties. The meals included unusual kinds of foods.

To solve some of the problems in the cities, the Romans built sewers to carry away waste. They also built **aqueducts.** These were systems of channels and pipes that carried water from springs and lakes into towns. Some were underground and some were located high on bridges. Some aqueducts are still used today.

Cities also had public baths. People of all classes visited the baths to take baths and socialize.

The Roman government provided entertainment for people at large public arenas. One of these was the **Colosseum,** where Romans watched **gladiators,** or trained warriors, fight to the death.

3. What problems did Roman cities face?

_____

_____

Chapter 13 The Rise of Rome

Glossary/After You Read

branch a part of something larger

civic relating to citizenship and its rights and duties

descendant a person related to a particular parent, grandparent, or other ancestor

fetch to go after and return with; to get

great-nephew the grandson of one's sister or brother

private school a school that charges students for admission

province a political division that is like a state of the United States

resentment anger

unrest disturbances or turmoil

Terms & Names

A. Write the letter of the term that matches the description.

_____ **1.** a piece of land surrounded on three sides by water

_____ **2.** a government in which people elect their leaders

_____ **3.** wealthy Roman landowners

_____ **4.** common Roman people

_____ **5.** lawmaking body of the Roman Republic

a. Senate

b. republic

c. plebeians

d. patricians

e. consuls

f. peninsula

B. In the blank, write the letter of the choice that best completes the statement or answers the question.

_____ **6.** The first settlers of Rome were the

     a. Greeks.   **c.** Latins.

     b. Phoenicians.   **d.** Gauls.

_____ **7.** Who made up the executive branch of the republican government?

     a. consuls   **c.** assemblies

     b. Senate   **d.** generals

_____ **8.** Rome fought the Punic Wars against

     a. Greece.   **c.** Spain.

     b. Gaul.   **d.** Carthage.

_____ **9.** Who was the leader who was made a dictator for life in 44 B.C.?

     a. Augustus   **c.** Romulus

     b. Sulla   **d.** Julius Caesar

READING STUDY GUIDE

____ **10.** What was the Pax Romana?

    a. a time of war in the Roman Empire   **c.** a time when plebeians had no political power

    b. a long period of peace in   **d.** a long period of rule by several generals
       the Roman Empire

Main Ideas

11. How did Rome's location near the Mediterranean Sea and the Tiber River influence its development?

_____

_____

12. Why Rome's location on the Italian Peninsula an advantage?

_____

_____

13. Why did patricians pass a set of laws called the Twelve Tables?

_____

_____

14. How were conquered people treated during the Roman Republic?

_____

_____

15. How did other cultures influence Roman religious beliefs?

_____

_____

Thinking Critically

16. Comparing and Contrasting Describe the aspects of the U.S. government that are modeled on the Roman republican government.

_____

_____

17. Forming and Supporting Opinions What do you think was the most important achievement of Augustus? Why do you think so?

_____

_____

Lesson 1 The Origins of Christianity

BEFORE YOU READ

In this lesson, you will read about the origins of the Christian religion.

AS YOU READ

Use this graphic organizer to sequence the events in the life of Jesus.

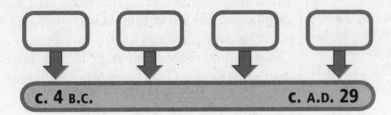

C. **4** B.C.   C. A.D. **29**

TERMS & NAMES

- **Jesus** A Jewish teacher who inspired the founding of Christianity
- **Gospel** An account of Jesus' life
- **disciple** A follower of Jesus
- **parable** A story with a moral
- **crucifixion** A form of execution on a cross practiced by the Romans
- **resurrection** Jesus' return to life after his execution

Christianity's Jewish Roots

(page 467)

How did Christianity build upon Jewish beliefs about the future?

In 63 B.C., the Romans took over Judah, which they called Judea. They ruled the Jews. Although the kings were Jewish, the Romans picked them.

At this time, many Jews hoped that a Messiah would come. Some hoped this Messiah would be an earthly ruler. Then they would be free to govern themselves. Some believed this ruler would be a descendant of King David.

1. What did some Jews believe the Messiah would do?

_____

_____

_____

The Life of Jesus

(pages 468–469)

Who did the disciples of Jesus believe he was?

Christianity grew out of the life and ideas of a Jewish teacher. His name was **Jesus.** We know about Jesus' life from the **Gospels.** Along with other writings, four Gospels make up the New Testament. It is the collection of Christian holy writings.

Jesus was a Jew. He was born in Bethlehem and grew up in Nazareth. Later, Christians would celebrate his birth on Christmas. He was raised by Mary and Joseph, a carpenter.

As a young man, Jesus became a traveling teacher. The New Testament says he cured the sick and lame. He did miracles, such as changing water into wine. His work attracted followers.

Jesus had 12 very close followers, or **disciples.** Some wondered if Jesus was the Messiah. Many Jews who followed Jesus thought so.

READING STUDY GUIDE

READING STUDY GUIDE CONTINUED

Jesus taught justice, compassion, and the coming of God's kingdom. He often taught using **parables.** They are stories with a *moral*. Three famous parables are the Good Samaritan, the Prodigal Son, and the Lost Sheep.

Jesus' most famous teachings were given in the Sermon on the Mount. He began it with beatitudes, or blessings. In this sermon, Jesus asked people not just to obey the law, but also to change in their hearts. He wanted people to love others—even their enemies. He also wanted people to live simply.

Jesus forgave people who broke religious laws. Many people thought only God could do this. Jesus also spent time with sinners who were outcasts. Most shockingly, some of Jesus' followers claimed that he was the Messiah.

2. Who did some people think Jesus was?

_____

_____

_____

_____

The Death of Jesus

(pages 470–471)

What belief about Jesus did Christians think made an afterlife possible?

Jesus made enemies among the Roman rulers and some Jews. The Romans did not like the claim that he might be the Messiah. That threatened their power. The claim also upset Jewish leaders.

According to the Gospels, Jesus' followers hailed him as king while he was in Jerusalem for the Jewish holiday of Passover. Jesus also criticized how the city's holy temple was run. These public challenges to Roman and Jewish authorities sealed Jesus' fate. Jewish leaders arrested Jesus. They turned him over to the Romans for punishment.

The Roman governor was Pontius Pilate. He ordered that Jesus be put to death by **crucifixion.** This meant he would hang on a cross until he suffocated. After Jesus died, a huge stone was put in front of his tomb.

Two days later, the Gospels say, some of Jesus' followers found the stone moved. The tomb was empty. Others said they saw Jesus. They had walked and talked with him.

Jesus' followers believed in his **resurrection.** To them, this proved that he was *divine*. They believed that Jesus had been willing to give up his own life for the sake of God's kingdom.

3. Why did Jesus' followers think he was divine?

_____

_____

_____

_____

READING STUDY GUIDE

Lesson 2 The Early Christians

BEFORE YOU READ

In this lesson, you will read about the work of early Christian leaders.

AS YOU READ

Use this graphic organizer to record details about Paul's life before and after he became a Christian.

Saul	Paul

TERMS & NAMES
- **Gentile** A non-Jew
- **missionary** A person who spreads his or her religion
- **Paul** Formerly Saul; a Jewish scholar who became a Christian leader
- **Epistle** A letter
- **persecute** To try to destroy

Jesus' Disciples

(pages 477–478)

What did Jesus' disciples do after his death?

Early Christian leaders, or apostles, were Jews. They believed in one God. They followed written law. The early church stressed sharing property. It also followed Jewish ideals of *charity*, helping prisoners, and common meals. Women and slaves wanted to join the church. This may be because the church taught that all its members were equal.

Jews divided the world into two groups—Jews and **Gentiles**, or non-Jews. Soon early church leaders began a debate. Some wanted to convert Gentiles to Christianity, too. Others did not want this.

At first the Romans ignored Christianity. Like the Christians themselves, they saw the religion as part of Judaism. Jewish leaders disagreed.

1. What Jewish ideas did the early Christian church follow?

_____

_____

_____

The Conversion of Saul

(pages 478–479)

What change did Saul undergo?

One Jewish leader was Saul. He worked hard to oppose the early Christian church. Saul was a Pharisee, or Jewish religious scholar. In Jerusalem, he tried to stop the spread of Christianity.

On the road to Damascus, Saul had a sudden change of heart. According to his own account, he came to believe that God had revealed Jesus to him. He came to believe that Jesus was the Messiah.

When Saul reached Damascus, he did not go after Christians. Instead, he joined them. He studied the new faith and began to convert Gentiles.

Saul's background helped him to convert a variety of people. He knew Jewish law very well. He had been born in Tarsus, a city in Asia Minor. It was heavily influenced by Greek culture. Saul spoke Greek. By birth, he was a Roman citizen. This allowed him to travel freely throughout the empire.

Saul had spent three years in Damascus. Now he was ready to become a **missionary,** or person who spreads his or her faith. To work among the Gentiles, Saul took a new, Roman name—**Paul.**

2. What made Saul become a Christian?

    _____

    _____

    _____

Paul's Journeys Spread Christianity

(pages 479–481)

Where did Paul travel, and why?

During Paul's lifetime, the Roman Empire experienced the Pax Romana, or Roman Peace. Rome's excellent roads were safe for Paul's widespread travels.

However, Paul's travels were not easy. He made three major missionary trips. Each one took several years. Paul wrote that he faced "dangers from rivers, dangers from bandits… dangers in the wilderness, dangers at sea."

For years, Paul and other apostles had struggled over whether Gentiles could become Christians without first becoming Jews. Paul said that becoming a Jew first was not necessary. He helped church leaders set up more limited rules for new Christians. This began to separate Christianity from Judaism. It also made the new religion more appealing to Gentiles. That helped it to grow.

Almost everywhere Paul went, he started a new church. He kept in touch with those churches through letters. Paul's letters explain Christian beliefs. They urge converts to live according to God's laws.

Paul's letters became an important part of the New Testament. They are called the **Epistles.** That is the Latin word for "letters." Paul wrote that believing in Jesus made all people one.

Eventually, Paul returned to Jerusalem. He was arrested by the Romans for bringing Gentiles into the Temple. After two years in prison, Paul demanded that he be tried before the emperor. That was his right as a Roman citizen. However, it had to happen in Rome.

Paul left for Rome in A.D. 59. He arrived in Rome the next year, and was kept under house arrest for two years more. During this time, he wrote several letters. The Romans had begun to **persecute,** or try to destroy Christianity. Paul probably died in Rome, maybe because of persecution.

Paul was the most important apostle. He helped spread the Christian church from Jesus' homeland to the wider world.

3. How did Paul's work separate Christianity and Judaism?

    _____

    _____

    _____

CHAPTER 14 | LESSON 3 Rome and Christianity

Lesson 3 Rome and Christianity

BEFORE YOU READ

In this lesson, you will read about how Rome reacted to Christianity.

AS YOU READ

Use this web to record details about how Roman views of Christianity changed.

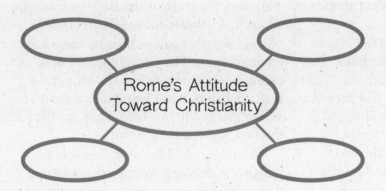

Rome's Attitude Toward Christianity

TERMS & NAMES

- **bishop** A local church leader
- **pope** The most important bishop
- **catholic** Universal
- **creed** A statement of beliefs
- **Trinity** The three persons of God; the Father, the Son, and the Holy Ghost

Rome's Policy Toward Other Religions

(pages 483–484)

Why was Rome hostile to Christians and Jews?
Rome was very tolerant of other faiths. However, Roman leaders would not allow alien religions to threaten their rule. Rome ended a Jewish revolt by destroying the Temple in Jerusalem.

As more Gentiles joined the Christian movement, Rome became alarmed. Christians would not worship the emperor. That was a challenge to Roman authority. Also Christianity appealed to women and slaves and this alarmed Rome, as did Christian talk about the coming of a Lord's kingdom that seemed to imply and end to the Roman empire.

The emperor Nero blamed the Christians for the fire that destroyed Rome in a.d. 64. Many Christians were persecuted and killed. Yet people kept converting. The ones who died for their beliefs became martyrs to other Christians. During the persecutions, Christians often hid in the catacombs, or underground cemeteries with secret passages.

1. Why was Rome worried about the spread of Christianity?

_____

_____

_____

_____

READING STUDY GUIDE

READING STUDY GUIDE CONTINUED

The Conversion of Constantine

(pages 484–485)

What was Constantine's policy toward Christianity?

In A.D. 306 Constantine became emperor of Rome. In 312 he was waging a key battle. In the middle of the fight, Constantine prayed for help. Later, he said he saw a cross in the sky. There were also the words, "In this sign, you will conquer." He ordered his soldiers to put the symbol of the cross he saw on their shields. Constantine won the battle.

Constantine immediately ended the persecutions of the Christians. In the Edict of Milan, he made Christianity an official religion. He returned property that had been taken from Christians. He built churches and put Christian symbols on coins. He made Sunday a day of rest. However, he did not formally convert until the very end of his life.

In 380, the emperor Theodosius made Christianity the official religion of Rome. Later, he closed all the pagan, or non-Christian, temples. He said, "All the peoples we rule shall practice the religion that Peter the Apostle transmitted to Rome."

2. What were the terms of the Edict of Milan?

_____

_____

_____

_____

Beginnings of the Roman Catholic Church

(pages 485–486)

What were some beliefs of the early church?

In the meantime, Christianity had developed a structure. A **bishop** led the church in each Roman city. Tradition says that Peter was Rome's first bishop. After his death, Rome's bishop became the most important one. He is called the **pope.** This was the start of the Roman Catholic Church. *Catholic* means "universal."

Some early bishops became known as the church fathers. They developed a Christian **creed,** or statement of beliefs. This creed features belief in the **Trinity,** or three divine persons united in one God. They are the Father, the Son, and the Holy Spirit.

An important Church Father was St. Augustine of North Africa. He wrote that God is present everywhere. The church also developed sacraments. Sacraments are rites such as baptism or *communion* based on the life of Jesus.

To live the Christian life and to celebrate the sacraments together, Christians began to form communities in the 300s. They were called monasteries. Christianity had grown from a small group to a powerful and wealthy religion.

3. Who is the most important leader of the Catholic Church?

_____

_____

_____

_____

CHAPTER 14 | The Birth of Christianity

Chapter 14 The Birth of Christianity

Glossary/After You Read

afterlife an existence or life thought to follow after death

alien from another country

astonishment sudden great surprise or wonder

charity the giving of help to people who are less fortunate

communion a celebration of Jesus in which Christians eat bread and drink wine

debate a discussion of opposite opinions; an argument

divine of, from, or like God

edict a statement by a ruler that has the force of law

moral the lesson taught by a story

waging conducting or carrying on

Terms & Names

A. If the statement is true, write "true" on the line. If it is false, change the underlined words to make it true.

_____ **1.** Each Roman city had Christian leader called a <u>pope</u>.

_____ **2.** The famous teacher had many <u>disciples</u>.

_____ **3.** Christians believe in Jesus' <u>resurrection</u>.

_____ **4.** As a Jewish leader, Saul would <u>convert</u> the Christians.

_____ **5.** The Gospels tell about the life of <u>Paul</u>.

B. Write the letter of the name or term that best matches the description.

____ **6.** one of the letters included in the New Testament

____ **7.** the most important apostle

____ **8.** the main figure of Christianity

____ **9.** something that is universal

____ **10.** a person who is not Jewish

a. catholic

b. Trinity

c. Epistle

d. Jesus

e. Paul

f. Gentile

READING STUDY GUIDE CONTINUED

Main Ideas

11. What religion did Christianity grow from?

_____

_____

12. Why do we know about Jesus' life and work?

_____

_____

13. How did Paul's view of Christianity help to spread the new religion?

_____

_____

14. What was the Edict of Milan?

_____

_____

15. What is the Trinity?

_____

_____

Thinking Critically

16. Understanding Cause and Effect How did Jesus make enemies among the Romans and some Jewish leaders?

_____

_____

_____

17. Making Inferences Why did the early church leaders call their church the "Catholic" Church?

_____

_____

_____

READING STUDY GUIDE

Lesson 1 An Empire in Decline

BEFORE YOU READ

In this lesson, you will learn what led to the split of the Roman Empire.

AS YOU READ

Use this cause-and-effect chart to list the effects of each of the causes listed.

Causes	Effects
Food shortages, wars, and political conflicts occur.	
Diocletian splits the empire.	
Constantine unites the empire.	

TERMS & NAMES
- **mercenary** a soldier for hire
- **Diocletian** Roman emperor who divided the empire in two
- **absolute ruler** ruler who has total power

Weakness in the Empire

(pages 495–496)

What problems weakened Rome?

After A.D. 180, several problems weakened the Roman Empire. The empire no longer could feed the growing number of people. This was due in large part to over-farming. This caused the land to become less fertile and produce fewer crops. Food shortages caused unrest among the people

The Roman Empire was running out of money. Many wealthy Romans spent their money on luxury goods from foreign countries. Many people did not pay the high taxes. As a result, the government did not have the money to pay for needed services.

Rome was often at war with Germanic peoples. The empire needed large armies to fight these people. To get enough people for the armies, the empire hired mercenaries from countries outside the empire. A **mercenary** is a soldier for hire. However, mercenaries did not have any *loyalty* to the empire. So the Roman army was not as strong as it once was.

As a result, the defenses along Rome's borders were weakened.

Many Romans no longer felt a civic duty to the empire. They pursued wealth instead. Between A.D. 235 and 284, the empire went through a series of emperors. Because the rulers changed so often, the government weakened.

1. What economic problems did the Roman Empire face?

_____

_____

_____

Diocletian Divides the Empire

(pages 496–497)

Why did Diocletian divide the Roman Empire?
The large size of the Roman Empire made it difficult to govern. The Emperor **Diocletian** reorganized the empire to make it easier to govern. He placed the army on the empire's borders to help defend it. He also tried to keep prices down on things such as bread to help the poor. Diocletian became more and more powerful and began making laws on his own. He became an **absolute ruler,** one who has total power.

To make running the large empire more *efficient,* Diocletian divided it in two. He ruled the Eastern Empire and appointed Maximian to rule the Western Empire. After 20 years, the two emperors stepped down. A civil war broke out, and four men fought for control.

2. Why did Diocletian divide the Roman Empire in two?

_____

_____

_____

_____

Constantine Continues Reform

(pages 497–498)

How did Constantine change the empire?
Constantine was one of the men who wanted to gain control. He became emperor of the West in A.D. 312. Twelve years later he also took control of the East. He reunited the empire and became the only emperor.

Constantine moved the capital of the empire from Rome to Byzantium, a city in what is now Turkey. Constantine beautified the city and renamed it Constantinople.

After Constantine's death, his three sons fought for control of the empire. But the empire was eventually permanently divided into eastern and western empires.

3. How did Constantine change the empire?

_____

_____

_____

_____

READING STUDY GUIDE

Lesson 2 The Fall of the Roman Empire

BEFORE YOU READ

In this lesson, you will learn what led to the end of the Roman Empire.

AS YOU READ

Use this chart to sequence the events that led to the end of the Roman Empire.

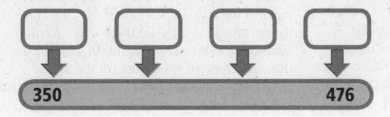

350   476

TERMS & NAMES

- **barbarian** people who lived outside the Roman Empire
- **nomad** people who move from place to place
- **plunder** to take things by force

The Two Roman Empires

(pages 501–502)

Why did the Western Roman Empire weaken?

The Eastern Roman Empire was stronger than the Western Roman Empire. Traders from Asia, Africa, and Europe passed through Constantinople. As a result, the Eastern Empire was wealthier than the Western Empire. The eastern cities were also larger and better protected.

Cities in the Western Empire were not as big or wealthy as the cities in the Eastern Empire. They were not near trade routes. They were not well *fortified,* making it easier for them to be attacked by tribes of people on the northern border of the Roman Empire. The cities in the Western Empire became more unsafe. As a result, many people left the cities, making them easier to attack.

1. Why were the cities in the Eastern Roman Empire wealthier than those in the Western Roman Empire?

_____

_____

_____

_____

Invading Peoples

(pages 502–503)

What groups moved into the Roman Empire?

Tribes along the northern borders of the Roman Empire took advantage of its weaknesses and attacked Roman cities. These groups of people were known as Germanic people. They all spoke languages that were from the language family called Germanic. The Romans looked down on these people. The Romans called them **barbarians.** At first, the term was used to describe anyone who lived outside the Empire. The word eventually had a negative meaning. It came to mean someone who was uncivilized. The Romans used the word to refer to **nomads.** These were people who moved from place to place.

In fact, Germanic peoples had a very complex culture. They were skilled metalworkers. Some had elected assemblies. War chiefs led their military.

As Rome began to decline, groups of armed nomads from Central Asia, called the Huns, threatened the nomadic people who lived along the borders of the Roman Empire. The Huns drove the Germanic people into Roman territory. The Germanic people looked for protection from the Roman armies. But the Romans viewed them as dangerous.

2. Who pushed the Germanic tribes along the borders of the Roman Empire into Roman territory?

_____

_____

_____

_____

The Fall of Rome

(pages 504–505)

How did the Western Roman Empire end?

Rome declined for many reasons. Government officials were corrupt and citizens were indifferent. In 410, a group of Germanic people called the Goths attacked and **plundered,** or looted, the city of Rome. The attack seriously weakened Rome.

The Germanic peoples then invaded what is now France, Spain, and northern Africa. The empire's army was too weak to protect against the invasions. Then in 445, the Huns began attacking cities in the Eastern Empire and then the Western Empire. In 476, the last Roman Emperor was taken off the throne. This date marks the end of the Western Roman Empire. Life in the empire changed. Roads were destroyed and trade declined. Germanic kingdoms arose on the Roman lands. The Church gained power. The Eastern Empire, however, continued for another thousand years.

3. What happened after the last Roman Emperor was taken off the throne?

_____

_____

_____

_____

READING STUDY GUIDE

Lesson 3 The Byzantine Empire

BEFORE YOU READ

In this lesson, you will learn how Christianity developed in the Eastern Roman Empire.

AS YOU READ

Use this chart to summarize information about the Byzantine Empire.

Justinian	
Split in Christian church	
Role of church in government	

TERMS & NAMES

- **Byzantine Empire** the Eastern Roman Empire
- **Justinian** emperor of the Eastern Roman Empire
- **Justinian Code** a uniform code of laws
- **Roman Catholic Church** the Christian Church in the West
- **Eastern Orthodox Church** the Christian Church in the East

A Continuing Empire

(pages 509–510)

How did the Byzantine Empire preserve Roman culture?

The city of Constantinople was originally named Byzantium. As a result, the Eastern Roman Empire became known as the **Byzantine Empire.** This empire lasted for about a thousand years after the end of the Western Roman Empire. The emperor of the Eastern Empire, like the one for the Western Empire, was an absolute ruler. Like the Western Empire, the Byzantine rulers tried to keep invaders out of their lands. But the invaders took over some of these lands.

The Emperor **Justinian** reconquered some of these lost lands. Justinian ruled from a.d. 527 to 565. During that time he rebuilt Constantinople. He built schools, hospitals, and churches. The most famous church was Hagia Sophia.

Justinian set up a committee to create a set of laws based on Roman law. He rewrote some of the laws to make them clear. This code of

laws was called the **Justinian Code.** It dealt with such things as marriage, women's rights, and criminal justice.

The Byzantines thought of themselves as part of the Roman culture. Students studied Latin and Greek and Roman history and literature. The Germanic peoples in the Western Empire blended Roman culture with their own. Much of Greek and Roman scientific knowledge was lost.

1. What was the Justinian Code?

_____

_____

_____

_____

READING STUDY GUIDE CONTINUED

The Church Divides

(pages 511–512)

Why did the Christian church split?

Religion developed differently in the Christian churches of the East and the West. Some of the differences were about religious practices. Other differences were about the authority of the emperor over church matters. In the western empire, the pope had the authority. But in the eastern empire, the emperor had authority over the head of the church.

The pope claimed authority over the church in both empires. In 1054, delegates of the pope tried to remove the eastern head of the church. This led the eastern church to refuse to recognize the authority of the pope.

Eventually, the Christian Church split in two. In the West the church became known as the **Roman Catholic Church.** In the East it bccame known as the **Eastern Orthodox Church.**

The pope claimed authority over emperors and kings. So the Roman Catholic Church was able to influence governments that were once part of the Western Roman Empire. Eventually, conflicts caused problems between the Church and kings and emperors.

The emperor had power over the government and over the head of the Eastern Orthodox Church. The Byzantine had more power than the emperors or kings in the West.

2. Why did problems develop between the Roman Catholic Church and the kings and emperors in the West?

_____

_____

_____

The Byzantine Empire Collapses

(pages 512–513)

What happened to the Byzantine Empire?

The Byzantine Empire continued to face threats from both the East and West. A religion called Islam started in Arabia. Muslim armies attacked Constantinople. The empire suffered attacks from the Ottoman Turks and the Serbs. All these attacks helped to weaken the Byzantine Empire. By 1350, only a small part of the Byzantine Empire remained. Then in 1453, Ottoman Turks captured Constantinople. This marked the end of the Byzantine Empire.

3. What event marked the end of the Byzantine Empire?

_____

_____

_____

_____

READING STUDY GUIDE

CHAPTER 15 | LESSON 4 The Legacy of Rome

Lesson 4 The Legacy of Rome

BEFORE YOU READ

In this lesson, you will learn about the legacy of the Roman culture.

AS YOU READ

Use a web diagram like this one to record information about legacies left by the Romans.

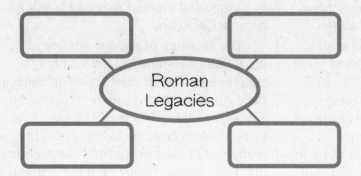

Roman Legacies

TERMS & NAMES

- **mosaic** a picture made from tiny pieces of colored stone or other material
- **bas-relief** a style of sculpture
- **epic** a long poem that tells about a hero's adventure
- **oratory** the art of public speaking
- **vault** an arch that forms a ceiling or a roof
- **aqueduct** a man-made waterway that brings water supplies to cities

---

Roman Culture

(pages 515–516)

How did Roman culture differ from Greek culture?

The Romans added Greek ideas about art and forms of writing to their own culture. Roman artists were skilled in making mosaics. A **mosaic** is a picture made from tiny pieces of colored stone or other material. Many mosaics show scenes of daily life. Although Romans modeled their sculpture on the Greeks, Roman sculptures did not show the ideal. Rather, they showed realistic portraits of individuals. The Romans borrowed a style of sculpture known as **bas-relief** from the Greeks. In this style, slightly raised figures stand out against a flat background.

The Greeks influenced Roman writing. One influence was the **epic.** This is a poem about a hero's adventure. The *Aeneid* by the poet Virgil is an example of a Roman epic. It is similar to the Greek epics the Iliad and the *Odyssey.*

The works of the Latin writer Cicero provide a picture of Roman life. Cicero's works also include speeches. Cicero was a master of **oratory,** which is the art of public speaking.

The Latin language spoken by the Romans became the basis of a group of languages known as romance languages. They include French, Spanish, and Italian.

1. How did the Greeks influence Roman writing?

_____

_____

_____

_____

READING STUDY GUIDE CONTINUED

Technology, Engineering, and Architecture

(pages 517–518)

How did Roman ideas about architecture and engineering influence builders throughout history?

Greek architecture influenced Roman builders. They found ways to improve the structure of buildings. They used arches, vaults, and *domes*. A **vault** is an arch that forms a ceiling or a roof. Roman improvements allowed Romans to build larger, taller buildings. Many buildings today use Roman ideas of design and structure. Romans developed a kind of concrete, which helped to create stronger buildings.

The Romans built **aqueducts** to bring water to cities. An aqueduct is a man-made waterway. Aqueducts supplied water to fountains, from which people brought water to their homes. Aqueducts are still found in lands that were once part of the Roman Empire.

Romans were famous for building many roads. In time, roads stretched from Rome throughout the empire. The roads helped soldiers move quickly. They also helped to increase trade, because people could move goods more easily.

2. How did a system of roads help the Roman Empire?

_____

_____

_____

_____

Religion and Law

(pages 518–519)

What legacies did Rome leave in religion and law?

The Roman Empire influenced religion and law. It was important in the spread of Christianity. The Roman Catholic Church eventually became powerful in Western Europe. The Eastern Orthodox Church became important in the Byzantine Empire. With both churches spreading Christianity, much of Europe and parts of Asia and North Africa became Christian.

The structure of the government of the Roman Republic influenced the U.S. government. The Roman senate influenced early Americans to set up their own Senate. The Justinian Code served as a model for many modern laws, including the right to own property. Citizens in the Roman Republic had the right to equal treatment under the law. This idea influenced many countries, including the United States.

3. Which element of the government of the Roman Republic influenced the U.S. government?

_____

_____

_____

_____

READING STUDY GUIDE

Chapter 15 Rome's Decline and Legacy

Glossary/After You Read

consult go to for advice

domes rounded tops or roofs that look like half of a ball

efficient functioning without waste of time, materials, or energy

fortified made strong against attack

limited restricted; not occurring often

loyalty faithful support

modeled created based on a model or example

negative lacking in positive qualities

preserve to maintain or protect from deterioration

tradition a belief of practice that is passed down from one generation to the next

Terms & Names

A. Complete the sentences below with a term from the Word Bank.

Word Bank		
mosaics	Eastern Roman Empire	oratory
Western Roman Empire	absolute ruler	mercenaries
barbarians		

1. To get enough people to fight the Germanic peoples, the Roman Empire hired _____.

2. During his reign, Diocletian gained more an more power and became a(n) _____.

3. The Romans referred to the Germanic peoples as _____, meaning that they were uncivilized.

4. The _____ became known as the Byzantine Empire.

5. Roman artists were skilled in making _____, which were pictures made from tiny pieces of colored stone.

6. Cicero was known for _____, the art of public speaking.

B. Circle the name or term that best completes each sentence.

7. To make it easier to run the Roman Empire _____ divided it in two.

   Diocletian   Justinian   Constantine

8. Emperor _____ moved the capital of the Roman Empire from Rome to Byzantium.

   Diocletian   Justinian   Constantine

READING STUDY GUIDE

9. The year 476, when the last Roman Emperor was taken off the throne, marks _____.

   the end of the Eastern Roman Empire   the end of Constantinople

   the end of the Western Roman Empire

10. The Emperor _____ was known for rebuilding Constantinople and setting up a code of laws.

    Diocletian   Justinian   Constantine

11. One improvement in building used by the Romans was the _____, an arch that forms a ceiling or a roof.

    vault   dome   mosaic

Main Ideas

12. Describe three reasons why the Roman Empire began to weaken after A.D. 180.

    _____

13. How did Diocletian try to make the empire easier to govern?

    _____

14. Why were Germanic peoples able to overrun the Roman Empire?

    _____

15. What issue led to the split of the Christian church in the East and the West?

    _____

16. How did the Romans influence languages?

    _____

Thinking Critically

17. **Comparing and Contrasting** How did the Western Roman Empire compare to the Eastern Roman Empire.

    _____

    _____

18. **Making Decisions** If you were an advisor to the emperors of the Western Roman Empire, what advice would you have given them to help strengthen the empire.

    _____

    _____